HANDLEY PAGE HERALD

G. COWELL

HANDLEY PAGE HERALD

JANE'S
LONDON · NEW YORK · SYDNEY
AN AIRLINE PUBLICATIONS BOOK

First published in the United Kingdom in 1980 by
Jane's Publishing Company Limited
238 City Road, London EC1V 2PU

In co-operation with
Airline Publications and Sales Ltd
Noble Corner, Great West Road, Hounslow, Middx

ISBN 0 7106 0045 3

Photoset by Method Limited, Woodford Green, Essex
Printed in Great Britain by Redwood Burn Limited
Trowbridge and Esher

Contents

Acknowledgements	*page* 6
Foreword by Capt Hedley G Hazelden	7
Introduction	11
Wanted - A DC-3 Replacement	15
A Marathon Venture	19
Turboprops v Pistons	24
Herald Flight Testing and Proving	31
On Tour	40
Royal Tour by Dart Herald	49
In Service - UK and Channel Islands Operators	53
In Service - Foreign Operators	86
Military Herald and Other Variants	103
Malaysian Ferry Flight	113
VIP Herald	116
Accidents	119
Airlines that Didn't Take Delivery	123
The Rolls-Royce Dart	140
Leading data	144
Herald Cross Reference Index	144
Production List	145
Herald Flying Hours and Landings	153

Acknowledgements

Compiling this acknowledgement was a strange task, for it aroused both sad and happy thoughts.

Those connected with the Herald project were only too willing to help in my research, for which I thank them most sincerely. On the other hand, their words revealed that Handley Page's brainchild was not destined to become a world-beater, as had first been thought, and it was with sadness they spoke about a sturdy aeroplane that never really stood a chance against its competitors.

My grateful thanks must go to Handley Page's former chief test pilot, Sqn Ldr H. G. Hazelden, who kindly consented to write the foreword, and to other one-time employees of the firm, including Don E. Westcott and Alex C. Morris, for invaluable data.

I am indebted to Sqn Ldr Norman Rose, who 'grew up' with the Malaysian military Heralds, for supplying little-known facts for one chapter, and to the airlines that have operated the type, in particular Capt Bernard Gardiner, David Hoyland and Roger Sweet of British Island Airways; Jeremy Keegan and Mrs Lyn Wilcox of British Air Ferries; Mr P. G. Walton of Air Anglia; Capt B. Cramp of British Midland Airways; Capt W. R. Bryce of Brymon Airways, and Arkia, Bavaria and Eastern Provincial Airways (1963) Ltd.

Special thanks are due to BAF and Capt John Woodhouse for allowing me to fly back to Southend from Malaysia on a Herald ferry flight, and to Malaysian Airline System for getting me out there!

Mr Mike Saggers of Lloyd's Aviation Department helped with details on Herald accidents. My thanks also go to Dart Herald (Support) Ltd, and especially to Mr M. J. Page and Mr T. S. Jones for allowing me to browse through their records. Further assistance came from Philip J. Birtles, Capt John Morris and from Philip Jarrett, who read through and corrected the manuscript.

Doubtless I have omitted someone who should be mentioned; if that is the case, my sincere apologies and belated thanks.

Foreword

by Capt H. G. Hazelden

When Graham Cowell asked me to write a foreword to his book about the Herald, it was a task which I accepted with considerable pleasure. As chief test pilot of Handley Page Ltd, the Herald was my main preoccupation for some 10 or 11 years. As I read Mr Cowell's extremely well-researched manuscript I was able, for the first time, to see the whole project in a more objective light than had hitherto been possible. That may sound a little surprising when I add that since leaving Handley Page in 1967 to become an airline pilot, I have flown not only the Herald but also its two competitors, the HS748 and the Fokker Friendship, on normal commercial operations. This experience, which is probably unique, has enabled me to compare three very similar aeroplanes in a way possible only to a few people.

All three were aimed at the 'DC-3 replacement' market, although 100 per cent success in this object would only have been possible with an aeroplane available in similar numbers and at a similar price to the old war-surplus Dakotas. However, even a small percentage of this huge market was a lucrative goal. At Handley Page the task was tackled by first asking every DC-3 operator, world-wide, what the requirements would be were they in a position to order a new aeroplane to their own individual specification.

This in 1952 produced the not unexpected preference for a machine with about 40 seats and powered by four piston engines. At that time the turboprop engine was still too new and unproven, and operators doubted whether it could match the reliability of the Dakota's piston engines, and also their own ability to service them properly with their often somewhat primitive resources. The four-engine preference was obviously for safety considerations.

With our long tradition of building large aeroplanes, passenger comfort was a prime consideration, and for this we had set the standards with the old HP42 and later the Hermes IV. This led us to favour a larger diameter fuselage than our competitors, which of course increased the tare weight. We could not visualise that the travelling public would accept the cramped and uncomfortable seating now commonplace for economy and inclusive tour travel. Possibly we failed to appreciate the unpleasant truth of modern business, that the consumer is seldom offered what he would like but only what the supplier can persuade him to accept; the only commodities offered therefore are those with most commercial advantage to the supplier. Alas, we were not going to sell to the public, but to the operators, and they had different ideas on what they could sell to the public.

Design studies indicated that, for the aeroplane we wanted to build, four engines of around 1,000 h.p. each would be needed. No suitable engine, either piston or turbine, existed. The Rolls-Royce R Da 6 was not considered adequate for a twin-engined machine, and no further development was proposed at that time. The decision was therefore taken to use four Alvis Leonides Majors, which were giving just over 800 h.p. and which were expected to be developed to higher powers in the reasonably near future. The single-row radial Leonides had been quite successful, but unfortunately its bigger double-row brother proved a disappointment.

By the time the first prototype Herald was completed in August 1955 the picture had changed dramatically. The Viscount had proved the Dart engine, and as a result most of the earlier piston engine protagonists were clamouring for a 'twin-engine Viscount'. There were also prospects of a higher-powered version of the Dart engine, and this, we felt, would make possible a future development of the Herald.

Owing to engine problems with the piston-powered Herald, it became clear that airworthiness certification of this version was becoming increasingly doubtful, and it was therefore necessary to proceed forthwith to the Dart Herald.

Another point which should be mentioned is the manner in which the Herald project was handled as a 'private venture'. It was in fact a collective private venture by the whole aviation industry, insofar as each subcontractor undertook the development costs of his own components. These costs, it was hoped, would be recovered by future sales of what was generally expected to be a world-beater. This, however, was not to be, and many others besides Handley Page were the losers.

What went wrong? In my opinion we failed to appreciate the potential of the turboprop engine in time, and we were too insistent on making our own ideal aeroplane. The greater physical size of the Herald compared with the HS748 and F-27 gave greater passenger comfort, but the detrimental effect on performance was its downfall. It was a bit slower and had less range than the others. The cramped cockpit showed up badly against that of the HS748 and, although the F-27 has an even smaller flight deck, it has greatly superior speed and performance to offset such design shortcomings.

It is not sufficient to say that the Herald failed because of the decision to build the piston-engined version or that the Dart Herald came too late. The HS748 was even later, yet it succeeded because its performance was better, and its flight deck made it more pleasant to operate.

The Dart Herald, with its light spring-tabbed controls, is the nicest one of the three to handle, but the lack of space to stow the multiplicity of books, manuals and paperwork regarded as essential to modern airline operations leaves much to be desired. After all, most of the time the autopilot is doing the flying, so pilots tend to opt for the most comfortable 'office' rather than the optimum flying characteristics. Airworthiness requirements ensure that any aeroplane will be easily controllable in every aspect of flight, so handling characteristics have little influence on the choice of an aeroplane for a specific operation.

However, performance in terms of speed, range and load-carrying have a very significant effect on operating economics, and the aeroplane which has advantages in such respects will in the long run be found most suitable for more varieties of operation, and hence become the more saleable product. There are other factors which affect saleability; for example spares availability, service back-up and ease of maintenance, but most of these factors are capable of improvement by efficient organisation. Basic performance, however, can seldom be improved without recourse to drastic and expensive modifications, such as the fitting of more powerful engines or structural changes which increase either weight or drag or both.

Of course, those of us who worked on the Herald wish our labours could have been crowned with greater success. We made a good aeroplane, but were unfortunate that other teams were able to produce machines which were slightly better. To those who are interested in what effort was expended, I commend them to this excellent account by Graham Cowell.

CAPT HEDLEY G. HAZELDEN
Aberdeen, December 1976

Introduction

In many respects Handley Page's winged workhorse was well-named. The dictionary defines a Herald as 'an officer whose duty was to proclaim peace or war, to challenge to battle, and to carry messages between sovereigns and princes'.

'Herald' can also mean to announce, to introduce, to usher in. In Handley Page's mind, their new airliner was designed to herald a new age of air travel, to break down barriers and earn profits for its operators. It also launched a full-scale war between opposing companies to capture a vast market where operators needed (or had to be told they needed) to dump their ageing Dakotas and get 'with it' by buying a modern, short range, small payload feeder airliner.

Handley Page's challenge was taken up, the main adversary being the Dutch Fokker company which, with foresight, was eventually to reign victorious with their brainchild, the F-27 Friendship.

The message was loud and clear. There was money to be made supplying the right kind of machine to the right people – but at the right time. Unfortunately, this was to be the Herald's downfall.

Sir Frederick Handley Page, the individualistic, autocratic, clear-thinking father figure of the company he founded, did not look far enough ahead. He tended to agree with those who made a fundamental miscalculation of the future market. In the early 'fifties, when the Herald was taking shape, some experts said that replacements for the DC-3 would be needed within five years. With 20 years' hindsight, one can safely say they were slightly off-beam!

'H.P.', as he was known, stuck to the four-engine formula, using a relatively new type of piston engine – the Alvis Leonides Major. The Herald started off on the wrong foot, and ultimately the company lost its balance. By 1956 it was obvious that the high maintenance and overhaul costs incurred by four engines was a great deterrent to potential and future airline operators. The Dutch did not fall into the same trap. Their first F-27 prototype flew with two Rolls-Royce Dart turboprops – one of the most successful and dependable powerplants created.

'H.P.' put his money into this 'free enterprise' project at an ever-increasing rate, in the hope of coming up with another money-spinner like the DC-3 or Viscount. But the F-27 got the orders, and the Herald had to be withdrawn and re-engined with two Darts before the customers would buy.

The piston-engined Herald took to the skies in August 1955, followed by its Dart-powered Dutch competitor three months later. The first Dart Herald did not fly until March 1958. Because of the advantages being reaped by its chief rival, the British Government took the unusual step of ordering three production aircraft for sales promotion and evaluation purposes.

The piston/turboprop debate came as a nasty jolt to 'H.P.' The Herald was destined to be his last venture, and steering it through many setbacks until its eventual entry into service, just before his death, took up most of his energy in the last ten years of his life, when his health was beginning to fail. Just before his death in April 1962, he had to swallow the bitter pill of the Herald failing to be chosen as Britain's close-support military transport - despite the RAF and Army being in favour of it. The decision made a mockery of free enterprise, which the government of the day had so strongly encouraged when it took office. The nationalisation of the British aircraft industry in the early 'sixties meant enforced amalgamations - with the Herald and many other aircraft as the victims.

The company had traditionally built big aeroplanes, but these need enormous sums of money and, normally, some government backing.

Sir Frederick, who always opposed groupings and nationalisation, rejected offers to merge with the big aircraft companies, mainly for the sake of his long-service employees. Had he been assured of a future for his firm, he would probably have agreed to a merger with Hawker Siddeley early in 1962, but with his death the chance faded away, as the company was as individualistic as its founder. His passing deprived the British aircraft industry and world aviation of one of its finest and most creative men. He was big in every way - in stature, character, imagination and natural good humour.

In another respect 1962 was a good time for Handley Page and the Herald. The dictionary reference to the carriage of messages between sovereigns and princes was strangely prophetic, for HRH Prince Philip chose Heralds for his 38,000-mile 11-country South American tour.

Handley Page, the first limited liability company incorporated in Great Britain to build aircraft, celebrated its diamond jubilee on June 17, 1969, but at this time the rapidly escalating development costs of its new Jetstream transport started to bite. The company's main creditors, Cammell Laird and Barclays Bank, injected £2.5 million into Handley Page, which saved the Radlett plant from shutting down. But this was to prove only a temporary reprieve, for on August 8 that year Handley Page went into voluntary liquidation. Eight days later a new company was formed - Handley Page Aircraft Ltd - for the sole reason of carrying on Jetstream production. Various other trials and tribulations were to occur before the fateful June 1, 1970, when both old and new companies finally ceased to exist - a sorry day indeed not only for Handley Page employees but for aviation generally.

In August Dart Herald (Support) Ltd was formed by Scottish Aviation Ltd of Prestwick and C. F. Taylor Ltd to take over all Herald spares and tools. This Wokingham-based company hopes it will have work for many years to come, keeping the Heralds flying.

Handley Page may be no more, but many former employees are making sure the name of their old firm never dies. During 1979 the Handley Page Association was formed with Godfrey Lee as president. To most members H.P. means more than baked beans or horse power, and they would like to help keep it that way.

Explained secretary Bryan Bowen, who joined Handley Page in 1959: 'The association has been formed to keep alive the memories of the H.P. company, its founder and its aircraft and to bring together all those - especially ex-employees - who still have an interest in the company and its achievements.' A regular newsletter is published, and plans are in hand to possibly save and restore H.P. aircraft.

'Although it is now ten years since H.P. closed down, there still appears to be considerable interest among ex-employees, both in the St Albans/Radlett area and further afield, as to the fortunes of the company's employees and its aircraft,' said Mr Bowen.

J. GRAHAM COWELL
Petts Wood, Kent

Wanted – a DC-3 replacement

In the early 1950s airlines began to have misgivings about the safety aspect of operating their ageing DC-3s indefinitely, despite the type's excellent record of reliable service. The venerable Dakota had established itself as the standard short-haul airliner around the globe; the problem was that no adequate replacement seemed to be in sight!

A world survey of all DC-3 operators, starting in 1952, showed a marked preference for a replacement having four piston engines, seats for about 40 passengers in a pressurised cabin, a maximum range of 1,000 nautical miles and a cruising speed of 200kt.

The Handley Page design team at Woodley, led by Edwin Gray, set about working on a private venture 'DC-3 replacement' late in 1952. The world-wide market survey showed that piston engines should power a new design if it was to attract orders in Australasia, Asia and South America, where restricted maintenance facilities for turboprop engines would be available at remote airfields.

Nearly every airline in Europe, Asia, Africa, Australia and South America was approached before the drafting of the Herald specification. Handley Page was convinced of the need, on the world's short range and feeder line services, for a workaday general-purpose transport of good money-making potential for the operator. It was shown conclusively that there was a pressing need among large and small operators for an airliner of a sturdy type for heavy duty on short to medium routes in varied climatic conditions. Handley Page representatives flew over the routes of many different airlines, and talked to executives, pilots, engineers and passengers on their home ground. This process of market appraisal had never before been carried out so thoroughly by on-the-spot survey, and it proved of immense benefit to future Herald operators. A thousand-and-one small points, often forgotten when the specification of a new aircraft is drawn up, were considered at the initial design stage, and it could be said that the Herald's design was outlined by the world's airlines themselves.

The 1952 survey showed that the four-engined formula was widely demanded as a safety feature. The knowledge that an aircraft has four rather than two power plants is obviously more comforting to passengers and crews alike, particularly at high aerodromes in the tropics, where twin-engined aircraft are liable to meet disaster if an engine fails on take-off. At the time, piston engines were preferred by most operators whose aircraft flew from smaller airfields with few facilities. The simple piston engine is not adversely affected either in performance or in economics by operation from high altitude tropical airstrips. However, in the middle of 1954 Handley Page did say that as propeller turbine engines became more developed and benefited from years of service experience, they expected the airlines to recognise their suitability for short-range operations. At the time the preference for piston engines was not as surprising as it seemed a decade later, for the Viscount and Fokker Friendship had yet to prove the greater merit of the turboprop. Additionally, smaller operators did not want to be guinea pigs for the development of a new and revolutionary power plant.

Writing in the spring 1954 Handley Page Bulletin, Grp Capt A. F. 'Bush' Bandidt revealed that for the past two years he had toured the world in a Handley Page Marathon to find out the re-equipment needs of airlines operating short- to medium-range aircraft.

He had asked the airlines the following simple question: 'What do you intend to use as a replacement aircraft when your present equipment finally wears out?' Bandidt received many answers, but in general they said they would fly an aircraft which would make money so long as they could raise the capital to buy it in the first place.

There were an estimated 15,000 Dakotas in existence at the end of the Second World War, and they changed hands at very low prices. Spares were plentiful. Many of the airlines that operated them came into being because of the post-war cheapness of cast-off military aircraft. Most were making a living of sorts, but they operated on a shoe-string, providing a small profit for investors and a livelihood for staffs, but unable to save money for re-equipment. It was vital that the Dakota replacements made money. For if they did not, the chance to re-equip would not recur, argued Bandidt.

'After talking to many airlines throughout the world', he wrote, 'it seemed to me that there was a common factor in the requirements of different operators, whether in the undeveloped areas of the tropics or in those countries already carrying a complicated network of routes.

'An aircraft built on the following lines is, I am sure, the answer to civil aviation's biggest re-equipment problem; it is the aircraft which will make money for every airline which has the good sense to buy it.'

Bandidt's formula for success is set out below:

> All-up weight, about 33,500lb. Payload over 350 statute miles, about 10,000lb. Standard tankage for 1,600 miles (still air range) with a corresponding reduction in payload. Take-off run over 50ft obstacle, 650 yards. Landing run over 50ft obstacle, 750 yards. Cruising speed 200 m.p.h. Stalling speed 75 m.p.h. Four piston engines.

Other essential factors in the specification included: All-metal, with a tricycle landing gear (forward-folding main undercarriage) having large diameter (34in) wheels with low (less than 50lb p.s.i.) tyre pressure, hydraulic operation of undercarriage, flaps and disc brakes, high wing with large waist-high loading doors, pressurised, thermal anti-icing and moveable forward bulkhead in passenger cabin to accommodate mixed load.

Regarding the choice of four engines, Bandidt said: 'Many operators have not yet made up their minds on the need for four or fewer engines. But one must be realistic about power plants generally.

G-AODE (c/n 147) and 'DF (c/n 148) first flew with four Alvis Leonides Major engines. The petal-type opening of the Leonides nacelle is shown here. (Handley Page)

'An airline cannot afford to buy beyond its pocket or experience. All engines have to be overhauled and, as they are very complicated pieces of ironmongery, they must be looked at often. A modern engine very rarely fails, but if it does, it must not affect the safety of the aircraft and it must be able to be rectified quickly and cheaply.

'In this regard, probably it is enough merely to emphasise that what can be done with a simple piston engine cannot be done with a more complicated alternative.

'After-sales service is a significant factor in the operators' quest for trouble-free use of his engines. The number of spare engines or power plants which he must hold, a distance from the manufacturer, must be kept to a minimum.

'These points have led the majority of operators to the conclusion that the piston engine still cannot be beaten for the simplicity and economy needed by this class of aircraft. This is a genuine view and is in no way concerned with the fact that propeller-turbine engines of suitable power do not exist at present for an aircraft of HPR3 configuration.'

Handley Page representatives were somewhat taken aback at what they found going on 'behind the scenes' in some foreign lands. 'Gifts' and bribery were commonplace in several countries in South America and elsewhere. The primitive flying fields and care-free manner of ground staff and flying crew were not the only worries they had to contend with!

Bandidt found that Brazil and Colombia were possibly the most air-minded countries on earth - an interesting conclusion, for airlines in both lands were to operate the Herald (q.v.) Bandidt reported that the Colombians knew what they wanted, could run an airline well and were efficient pilots and mechanics. But no ordinary aircraft was needed to meet the exacting demands of flying out of aerodromes like Bogota (8,000ft above sea level) and La Paz, Bolivia (14,000ft).

Bandidt's efforts eventually paid off. Airlines told him the Handley Page project was warmly welcomed, as at last an aircraft company had come to them, the people who have to fly the aeroplanes, to ask what was required.

A Marathon Venture

The Herald's origins can be traced back to 1944, the wartime Brabazon Committee's type 5a requirement for a small 14-seat feeder airliner, and Miles Aircraft Ltd's design to specification 18/44, which covered the need for a post-war British feederliner for internal services.

George Miles' first project, the M56, was a highly streamlined high-wing monoplane powered by two Rolls-Royce Merlin 24s, seating 24 passengers, and having a tailplane with endplate fins and rudders.

The proposal was not adopted by the Ministry. Later that year Miles started work on the smaller M60 – later to become the Marathon. The M60 was also a high-wing monoplane with a twin-finned tail, but its power plant was four 330 h.p. de Havilland Gipsy Queen 71 engines.

The first prototype was completed in 14 months, and made its maiden flight at Woodley on May 19, 1946, piloted by K. H. F. 'Ken' Waller, Miles' chief test pilot. It featured triple fins and rudders, and was shown at the SBAC display at Radlett in September of that year, and again in 1947, when it was registered G-AGPD.

Unfortunately this machine crashed at Amesbury on May 28, 1948, just before Marathon production at Woodley was taken over by Handley Page (Reading) Ltd after the Miles firm hit financial troubles and went into liquidation. The remaining prototype, plus jigs and Miles' Reading factory, came under the control of Handley Page when the company took over the Miles firm. They eventually built 40 Marathons under the designation HPR1.

The third machine, G-AHXU, was a development aircraft for the proposed M69 powered by two 1,101 e.h.p. Armstrong Siddeley Mamba 502 turboprop engines. It became the Marathon 2, and Hugh Kendall flew it for the first time on July 23, 1949. Loaned to the Ministry of Supply as VX231, the Mamba Marathon had the distinction of being the first turboprop aircraft to fly with reverse-pitch propellers (de Havilland) which cut its normal landing run by half.

This unique machine had its Mamba power plants replaced by two 870 h.p. Alvis Leonides Majors with 'petal' opening cowlings projected for the HPR3 Herald. It flew from Coventry with the designation HPR5 from March 1955 until 1958, and was then fitted with the Armstrong Siddeley P181 engine for a further spell of development flying, finally being broken up in October 1959.

Miles had been working on a scaled-up version of the Marathon when the firm collapsed. This was the M73, with 4,500 h.p. Alvis Leonides engines, and was intended to fly late in 1948 or early the following year. The Handley Page design team used it as a basis for the HPR3.

Originally proposed during 1953, the HPR3 resembled a bigger Marathon. It had a high, straight-tapered wing and triple fins and rudders. Span was 90ft,

In 1954 the HPR5, VX231, a twin-engined flying test-bed, enabled the Leonides Major engines to be tested by Alvis. Clover-leaf cowlings opened wide to give easy access for maintenance. The engines were fitted in replicas of HPR3 nacelles. (Handley Page)

there was seating for 36 passengers, and power was supplied by four 870 h.p. Alvis Leonides Major piston engines.

On January 18, 1954, the Handley Page board decided to order two HPR3 prototypes to be constructed at Woodley. They also agreed to the spending of £1 million over the next three years, plus just over another £500,000 for tools and jigs. This represented a break-even figure for 75 machines. The name Herald was finally chosen from about a dozen possibilities, and revealed at a cocktail party given by Sir Frederick at the Air League headquarters on August 31, 1954.

By early 1955 the basic design had been 'cleaned up', and the three fins and rudders had made way for a large single unit. The original large ailerons were replaced by smaller ones with lift spoilers inboard; this left room for even larger-span slotted flaps.

A high wing layout was chosen for the ease of loading it allowed and for comfort in hot conditions. Passengers have an unrestricted view from the windows, and in the tropics the shade from the wing and the resultant cooling of the cabin are obviously welcome. The high lift wing and large Fowler-type flaps, coupled with the large fin and rudder, gave a good control at low speeds for short take off and landing (STOL).

The first of two prototypes, G-AODE (c/n 147), was registered in the summer of 1955 and made its 30-minute maiden flight on August 25 that year. Right from the start it was clearly a pleasant aeroplane to fly, said Sqn Ldr H. G. Hazelden, the Handley Page chief test pilot, who was at the controls on that first lift-off.

'I never knew our runways were so long; take off and landing were very short indeed,' he said afterwards. With him on the flight was Mr R. J. Davies, chief aerodynamicist of Handley Page (Reading) Ltd.

The rapid construction of the prototype – begun only 15 months previously – had reached a spectacular conclusion earlier in August, when the near-finished

G-AODE (c/n 147) rolled out of the hangar in the livery of Queensland Airlines of Australia. It sported a dark blue cheat line with QAL insignia on the nose and the airline's name painted under the fuselage windows. (Handley Page)

aircraft was dismantled, taken by road from the company's Woodley factory to its aerodrome at Radlett and reassembled there in 150 working hours.

The road journey necessitated the removal of all major components. The fuselage, reduced to little more than an empty shell, travelled on a two-wheel trailer and was joined to its vehicle by its own nose undercarriage mounting. The wing was divided into five sections. Fin, rudder, tailplane, elevators, flaps ailerons, undercarriage, engines, airscrews and cowling petals all made the trip as separate units.

At that stage it was almost complete externally except for the propellers and engine cowling petals. The simple, straightforward construction of the Herald was amply demonstrated. The following week all essential services were installed, and much of the cabin equipment and furnishings. A fortnight after the Herald's arrival at Radlett, pre-flight testing had begun.

On hearing of the Herald's maiden flight, Capt Norman Croucher, London manager of Australian National Airways, which then had an order for a large fleet, said: 'My company, responsible for carrying many passengers and a great deal of freight across the Australian continent, has been looking forward eagerly to the first flight of the Herald. I think the Herald, in its class, will cope effectively with the rapidly growing demands made on our air services'.

Sadly, the piston-Herald was already outdated when it first took to the air, and the decision to change power plants was not taken for another 21 months – crucial months that allowed the Fokker Friendship to pick up orders.

The Herald's first public appearance was at the 1955 SBAC display at Farnborough, when it appeared in Queensland Airlines colours. Late in 1954,

G-AODF (c/n 148), the second prototype, with the HP crest visible on the nose.

months before the prototype's first flight, the Australian airline became the first operator to order the Herald. G-AODE then began a 'low profile' flight test programme, leaving the limelight to the important Handley Page Victor bomber. It achieved C of A clearance on July 20, 1956. After the SBAC show in September 1955 development flying proceeded apace. A few problems did crop up, one of which was a lack of elevator power for landing with the c.g. forward, (*see* Chapter 4), cured by fitting a larger tailplane and elevator. A tendency for the fin to stall at high angles of sideslip at low speeds was rectified by adding a dorsal fin. During large angle sideslips at slow speeds, some buffeting was experienced on the elevator owing to local stalling at the tailplane root. This was eliminated by fitting an 'inverted slot' to a small span at the root of the tailplane leading edge.

There were two important reasons why four 870 h.p. piston engines were chosen. There were no suitable British piston engines of sufficient power to allow a twin installation, and it was impractical to buy foreign power units. 'Outback' areas were not ready for sophisticated turbine engines.

The second prototype, G-AODF, took to the air nearly a year after the first, on August 3, 1956, and appeared at the 1956 and 1957 Farnborough air shows. G-AODE was grounded in June 1957 to become the prototype conversion for the twin Rolls-Royce Dart Herald. In 2½ years' flying the two Leonides Heralds clocked up 440hr in the air.

At a press visit to Woodley during 1955, Handley Page sales manager Gp Capt Richard Collard said the Herald had four engines for safety. On such an aeroplane, he claimed, the loss of one engine was no more than an incident.

'They are piston engines to enable the owner and the operator to make money,' said Collard, who joined Handley Page in 1953 after leaving the RAF with 3,000hr on 45 different types to his credit.

'It is no use saying that local services can be operated by a larger line in its spare time, on the side, and that it can make a loss and make it up on the long hauls. If that were so, then aviation would slowly die over a great part of the globe. Local services – branch lines – can be operated with profit; but only if you have the right aeroplane.' It was Collard who first called the Herald a 'branchliner'.

'What we must think of are those areas of North and South America, of Africa and of Australasia, where transport is an essential part of the life of the community and where everybody flies,' he pointed out. 'In other words, one must consider this problem more from the point of view of, shall we say, an advanced, air-minded Peruvian Indian rather than a pedestrian and largely earthbound European.'

Collard said that more than one operator had suggested that the plane should have a tailwheel, as 'the nosewheel may get damaged on my very rough airfields and I believe we can always land shorter with a tailwheel.' But the ease of taxiing and of loading and unloading with a flat platform, and comfort when sitting in the stationary aircraft, outweighed the other points with the majority of operators.

Turboprops v Pistons

The Herald suffered considerable from the early decision to persevere with piston engines. By 1956 it was clear that many operators were having second thoughts about the choice of piston power, and the appearance of the Rolls-Royce powered Viscount and Friendship made some Herald customers decline to accept the piston-engined Herald.

The reason was the growing reliability and unquestionable simplicity of turboprops. Rolls-Royce produced a further development of the Dart engine – the RDa7 – giving a 2,100 h.p. which was considered just right for a twin Dart version of the Herald. As even smaller airlines shifted their allegiance from piston to turboprop, Handley Page decided, during 1957, to replace the four Leonides Majors of the HPR3 with two Darts – the first turbine engine to enter airline service.

The first prototype was thus withdrawn for modifications. As well as the engine change, the fuselage was increased in length to seat 44, cabin pressure was upped to 4.2 p.s.i. and the all-up-weight to 39,000lb. The modified machine, now designated HPR7, flew on March 11, 1958, from Woodley. The Dart 527 turboprops were installed about 30″ further outboard than the inner Leonides had been. The original undercarriage position was kept, and a highly asymmetric engine nacelle shape thus resulted. A short inverted slot was fitted at the tailplane edge root to smooth out the airflow over the elevator, and another major alteration was the addition of a large dorsal extension to the fin. By August 1958 the aircraft had flown nearly 200hr, and was considered to be sufficiently developed to obtain a C of A. G-AODE was awarded a preliminary C of A just over five weeks after its conversion, by which time the second prototype had also been ear-marked for conversion.

It was a wonderful aircraft to fly – even smoother and faster than the earlier version and with superior take off and landing performance.

Unfortunately, disaster was just around the corner. On a flight to the Farnborough air display from Woodley on August 30, the white, crimson and beige prototype was written off in a forced landing near Godalming, Surrey.

Piloted by Hazelden, and with Ray Wood as observer, G-AODE was flying at 6,000ft and having its photograph taken in company with a crescent-wing Victor bomber. Suddenly the low pressure turbine wheel of the starboard Dart burst and a large fragment cut through two of the engine bearers and severed the fuel line, causing a catastrophic fire. The flames melted the nacelle off in about two minutes, and it fell away, complete with engine. The fire extinguisher had little effect, and Sqn Ldr Hazelden, who was at the controls, lost height and tried to make a crash landing.

The aeroplane started to pitch, and he thought it might break up. When the engine fell away there was a violent roll, and he was only just able to recover

A tragic loss for Handley Page – the prototype burns out in a field near Godalming, Surrey, after a forced landing. G-AODE (c/n 147) was on its way to Farnborough for the 1958 air show. (Handley Page)

control. Fuel pouring from the tanks was feeding the flames, which in turn caused part of the tailplane to come away.

After scraping beneath some high tension cables, which the tip of the fin actually struck, Hazelden managed to touch down wheels-up in a stubble field at about 150 m.p.h. The Herald crossed a ditch into the next field and struck a large tree stump which tore a hole in the fuselage just behind the cockpit. Through this all nine occupants, including Hazelden's wife, rushed to safety.

The whole drama lasted about five minutes. Although it was obviously a severe set-back, the Herald was completely exonerated. The small component in the engine was one of a faulty batch and the weakness in the RDa7 was not present in earlier Darts.

The accident proved the robust character of the airframe and the advantages of the sandwich multiple-load path construction of the wings, using the fail-safe principle. Already the wing was expected to give 17 years' trouble-free service, and no official limit had been set on the life of the pressurised fuselage. Sqn Ldr Hazelden was given a gold watch for his outstanding feat of airmanship, while the other eight occupants each received a photograph of the Herald airborne just before its engine failed.

Hazelden recalls: 'We wanted to get some press publicity for the Herald at

Farnborough, so we were flying it in over the weekend, as the show started on the Monday. I took off from Reading, with John Allam in a Victor bomber from Radlett who was going to formate with us and a Hastings, carrying a party of photographers.

'The Victor nearly fell out of the sky trying to keep in formation, while the Hastings was going flat out. They were not very compatible when it came to flying in formation.

'My wife was with me, as I had been getting home late on several nights beforehand. I suggested she came down to Reading to make things simpler, and flew with me in the aeroplane. While in loose formation, we heard a bang and wondered "Christ, what was that?" I saw the fire and realised we were in a bloody serious situation.

'I carried out the fire drill, but there was only one fire extinguisher per engine. It doused the flames a bit, but then they came up again. I was in a partially shocked state. It was a terrible effort to remember what to do and the right order of doing it.

'We weren't going to fly very long at 6,500ft. I picked out the field eight or nine miles away. Then we rolled badly to starboard, and I thought this was it – the wing was going to come off. Then the controls responded, and we levelled off. We were still in business. I didn't use any flap.'

Hazelden said that after they had landed he realised the flames had been so strong they had burnt off the tailplane. The port wing and engine were later salvaged – in fact, the engine flew again in another aircraft.

When I told Sir Frederick about the crash', said Hazelden, 'he replied: "These things have happened before." He was a great old man.'

'A similar engine failure occurred in a Viscount sold to America. Rolls-Royce had transferred the manufacture of the Darts from Derby to Glasgow, and both faulty components were traced to the same hardening batch made in Glasgow'.

The second prototype conversion was nearly complete. It took to the skies on December 17, 1958, and received its C of A on December 31. Very little flying was needed before this second Dart Herald was ready for extensive demonstration tours, which started in April 1959 (q.v.).

This aircraft was later brought up to Series 200 standard by adding 42in to the cabin length and installing high density seating to take 56 passengers. It resumed flight testing on April 8, 1961, and in August was fitted with a nose radome, registered G-ARTC and repainted in Maritime Central Airways' colours for a 'brand new' appearance at that year's SBAC show.

In May 1957, it was decided to undertake parallel production of both the Dart-engined Herald and for the version powered by four Leonides piston engines. The manufacturer claimed that in many areas, especially remoter regions, the Leonides version would prove more suitable. It would score in very hot countries and in operations from small, high altitude airstrips in difficult terrain.

The Dart Herald, 70 m.p.h. faster, was more suited to fast branchline services in developed areas. Handley Page also expected its low purchase price,

£175,000, to be well received. The manufacturers thought the similarity of piston and turboprop Heralds would appeal to airlines with mixed operations. The four-engined variant would operate in particularly difficult conditions, while the Dart Herald would be perfect for more sophisticated routes where greater speed was more important for passenger appeal.

However, increasingly wide acceptance of the Rolls-Royce Dart led to the piston alternative eventually being dropped. Turboprops provide economic operating costs on short-range work.

Other provisional orders for the original version were placed by Lloyd Aero Colombiano and British Aviation Services Ltd. By April 1955 a total of 29 Leonides-powered Heralds had been ordered by overseas operators, doubtless encouraged by the Herald's operational economy of less than 1½d per passenger mile, or 1s 3d per ton mile.

The Herald, Friendship and Russian Antonov An-24 which made its maiden flight in the spring of 1960, are of similar and distinctive layout. All have been designed for medium to short haul routes in regions where servicing and airfield conditions may be primitive.

The high-wing layout allows easy access to the passenger cabin. The Herald's nose resembles that of the Viscount, and from the exterior is difficult to distinguish from the Friendship for the uninitiated. The Friendship is, however, a sleeker-looking machine, its nose being similar to that of the Dakota.

THE F-27

Few would argue that if any one aeroplane has come close to being that elusive 'DC-3 replacement', the Fokker-VFW Friendship must be the one. It is the free world's largest selling turboprop commercial transport. The Dart Mk 528 was chosen for the initial production versions, and to date, about 700 F-27 Friendships have been sold.

The design of a DC-3 replacement was first considered by Fokker in 1950. By September 1953 it had finalised as the F-27 around two Rolls-Royce Darts. Construction began on prototypes paid for by the Netherlands Institute of Aircraft Development, the first of which, PH-NIV, flew on November 24, 1955, at Schiphol, followed by the second in January 1957.

Fokkers built an aeroplane to suit the engines – a policy in which Handley Page did not believe. Instead, they thought its comfort would sell the Herald. Admitted Hazelden: 'We blundered badly. People are only offered what advertisers can persuade them to accept. Two things prevented us from selling – we had no support from the Government or national airlines, whereas the F-27 appeared with the apparent backing of KLM, and it had superior performance.'

The F-27 went into service (with Aer Lingus) at the end of 1958. The Irish airline was the first non-Dutch carrier to order the plane, and had stated when ordering their Friendship fleet: 'We realised that to operate 60-seater aircraft half full once a day was not as economic a proposition as operating a 30-seater sold to capacity twice a day'.

In April 1956, Fairchild in America signed an agreement with the Dutch aircraft company to build and market the Friendship in the USA. The first Fairchild machine was flown on April 12, 1958. Dutch production machines can be identified by Mark numbers, while those of Fairchild (later Fairchild Hiller) by F-27 or FH-227 designations.

Fokker proudly announced in 1962 that its Friendship, in only three years, had earned more profit and praise than any other aircraft employed on short- and medium-haul routes. In three years and more than 500,000 flying hours, claimed Fokker, it proved its effectiveness more fully, more consistently and to more airline operators than any other aircraft since the DC-3. Airlines in all continents also reported sharp increases in traffic following the Friendship's introduction on their routes - a sure indication of its passenger appeal.

All this was too much for the poor Herald, which, in the years to come, was to meet with little commercial success. While sales of the F-27 continue, only 50 of all Herald variants were built.

An initial production batch of 10 Heralds was laid down in 1959. The first of these was G-APWA, a Series 100 44-seater demonstration aircraft with the same cabin length as the two prototypes. Only three more of these short-fuselage machines were built (G-APWB, 'WC and 'WD). In June 1959 the first order for the new Herald was placed by the British Government. They bought the three Series 100s for use on the 'Highlands and Islands' services of BEA.

The rest of the initial production batch (the 'Whisky' series) were built as Series 201 machines for Jersey Airlines. Deliveries were scheduled to start in June 1961, by which time the manufacturers had obtained letters of intent for 16 Heralds from airlines in Brazil and Argentina, including one for seven aircraft from VASP. So far Handley Page had ploughed £4 million into the private venture Herald project.

In September 1961 it was announced that a second batch of 25 Heralds was being laid down. The 22nd production Herald was the first to have a strengthened undercarriage which increased permitted all-up weight to 43,000lb.

Increasing demand for Heralds in the early 'sixties led to a second production line being opened at Cricklewood, space no longer being available at Woodley, which was to be vacated by the end of 1962. At this time the Reading and Cricklewood design departments were merged. Some 30 Series 200s had been delivered by mid-1966, when production of the Herald began to be transferred to Radlett from the Cricklewood works, which were being sold for redevelopment.

In July 1962, a new subsidiary company, Handley Page (Leasing) Ltd, was formed with a capital of £25,000. It owned Heralds and leased them to operators pending delivery of their own machines.

It was from a Series 200 that paratroops of the 22nd Special Air Service achieved a new British Commonwealth free-fall record in 1962, jumping from

34,350ft. Eight men jumped from the standard civil Herald, delaying the opening of their parachutes until they were only 2,000ft above ground. It is not generally known that one of the SAS men died in the attempt, when he failed to pull his rip-cord. Hazelden, who flew the Herald up to that lofty altitude, recalls: 'These men were used to doing their own thing. They had been doing free-fall parachuting, and got to hear a Herald had been up to 31,000ft. We were approached and asked if we would be interested in helping them to push the record up.

'I think the highest they had jumped from was 12,000ft. The aircraft was only altered by taking off the passenger door and fitting it with an oxygen system. Unfortunately the operation became a little rushed, and it was decided there was no time for a practice drop. So they went for the record instead. It was the highest the Herald had ever flown. The average error from the drop zone was only 600 yards.'

In 1962 the Herald order book showed machines for Itavia, Jersey Airlines, North-South Airlines and Maritime Central Airways. Come 1963 the version had been selected by the following operators: Jersey Airlines (six), BUA (one), Nordair (two), Maritime Central (two), Itavia (two), Cambrian (one), Eastern Provincial Airways (two), Arkia (two) and the Royal Jordanian Air Force (two).

In 1964 the order book stood as follows: BUA (seven), Itavia (two), Eastern Provincial Airways (four), Arkia (two), Globe Air (four), Cruz Airways (two) and Royal Jordanian Air Force (two).

G-AODF (c/n 148) later became G-ARTC. Here the Herald demonstrates its ability as a paratroop aircraft. (Handley Page)

By mid-1965 orders from 14 operators totalled 52 aircraft. Export machines comprised 88 per cent of all Heralds and spares ordered to that date – the value of which totalled £15 million. Six months later the figure had increased to 57 Heralds ordered by 17 different operators. No fewer than 51 of those were destined for overseas customers. Exports claimed a staggering 90 per cent of all private-venture Heralds and spares ordered, which, by December 1965, were valued at £18 million.

In the first three years of service, Heralds logged nearly 10 million miles and more than 50,000 landings with an unsurpassed safety record. By the end of 1964 some 35 of the type had flown about 70,000hr in service with ten operators.

Herald flight testing and proving

By mid-November 1955 the Leonides Herald G-AODE had flown 50hr during 58 flights. Sqn Ldr Hazelden produced a report six weeks after the Herald's first flight, saying no difficulties had been experienced taxiing on tarmac and at the grass airfield at Woodley under weather conditions varying from heavy rain to strong crosswinds.

On take-off, at weights of up to 29,000lb, only a slight pull was needed to unstick at speeds of 60-80kt. Trimming was easy, and there was no tendency to swing when taking off into wind. Rudder became effective at speeds as low as 30kt, and distance to unstick was 300-400 yards.

When simulating engine failure on take-off, the starboard outer engine was suddenly throttled back, before retracting undercarriage or flaps, at speeds down to 75kt. Control was maintained and climb-out continued on the other three engines. With both starboard engines feathered and full climbing power (maximum continuous power) from both port engines, no difficulty was found controlling the aeroplane at speeds down to 105kt in asymmetric flight.

The Herald exhibited a high degree of stability in all three planes. There was no tendency for 'wallowing' or 'Dutch rolling' in turbulent conditions, sometimes associated with types with a high degree of stability in the lateral and directional planes. It was possible to fly 'hands and feet off' for considerable periods.

Commenting on general handling, Hazelden said that on first flights the controls were purposely made heavy. In later flights they were progressively lightened, proving completely effective. Ailerons and elevators were pleasant to handle.

At a weight of 28,000lb, power-off stalls were performed with undercarriage up and flaps set to 'up', 'take-off' and 'fully down'. Stalling speeds were 78, 65 and 59kt respectively. Observed Hazelden at the time: 'There was practically no pre-stall warning. Some further developments will be necessary to provide warning of the approach to stall." The landing circuit could be made quite comfortably at 95-100kt, and final approach was at 80-85kt, when full landing flap could be lowered. There was a noticeable nose-down change of attitude when flaps went fully down, giving a fine, unobstructed view of the runway. All-round view from the cockpit was excellent. Brakes, with anti-skid devices, were smooth and powerful, allowing a landing run of a mere 400-500 yards.

Except for a few minor faults, the engines proved trouble-free. Response to the throttles was excellent, reported Hazelden. 'Throttle and pitch lever alignment is extremely good throughout the whole range of movement," he observed. This made simultaneous control of the four engines much easier than was often the case on prototype aircraft.

Hazelden's general conclusion was that the Herald was easy and pleasant to

Dart Herald instrument panel.

fly, with enough control to cope with any emergency.

During its second 50hr of flying an extensive flight test programme was undertaken. This included various performance measurements in level and climbing flight and others covering take-offs and landings.

The second prototype was used to prove the cabin pressurisation and de-icing systems, and for tropical trials followed by demonstration flights overseas. (The first aircraft was not pressurised). It was reported in the summer of 1956 that G-AODF would afterwards be put into service with an airline for some months.

It was then current airline practice on certain local-service flights to cut time spent on the ground by stopping only the port engines while passengers were getting in and out. Using its steerable nose wheel, the Herald could taxi on starboard engines only, allowing the port engines to be stopped and started while taxiing.

Structural tests were carried out on a complete Herald fuselage at the Radlett test plant, and another fuselage was pressure-tested at the design and production unit at Woodley. The Herald was not highly pressurised – the maximum being 3.35 p.s.i. The tests were designed to measure stress levels in the fuselage under pressure loads, and to this end it was covered with more than 5,000 strain gauges and the air pressure raised in 0.5 p.s.i. steps. The differential was raised to 4.50 p.s.i., well above operating levels. For testing at pressures above 2 p.s.i., the fuselage was filled with cans which had a controlled air leak, to stop explosive decompression if a minor structural failure arose.

Like most aircraft of its type, the Herald has a two-man flight deck. Vision over the nose from either of the pilots' seats is so good that, on the ground, objects less than 10ft away can be seen. Five flat windscreen panels give wide vision from wingtip to wingtip. A pleasing feature, from the passenger viewpoint, is the large oval windows. The vast, almost square fin resulted from the need to control asymmetric flight with two engines stopped while keeping this surface within Dakota hangar height.

Unlike the Herald, which has twin nosewheels, the Friendship has only one.

The Dart Herald

One of the prototype Dart Heralds was to have been put to work with Derby Aviation for several months' intensive flying during the airline's busy season. The airline, the forerunner of British Midland Airways, operated Handley Page Marathons at the time.

Handley Page had the advantage of know-how gained from extensive development and flying with the piston-engined Herald, but a fuselage underwent a trial by water in an RAE Farnborough tank at 6 p.s.i. Artificially-produced cracks appeared at 3.35 p.s.i. and, following 60,000 pressure cycles, again at 4.2 p.s.i. The fuselage was finally pressurised in the tank until it failed at 9.61lb. Owing to the fail-safe nature of the wing, the fatigue life was expected to be at least 50,000hr - 17 years of use at 3,000hr a year.

Pressurisation was set at 4.2 p.s.i., equivalent to a cabin altitude of 8,000ft when flying at 20,000ft. The water tank programme yielded results that made production Heralds the safest new British aircraft to enter airline service, with an indefinite fatigue life.

Perhaps the main design feature of the tail was its fluted skin, which permitted a simplified internal structure and had no effect of drag. At an early design stage, a research specimen tailplane was used to investigate this simplified form of structure. A series of tests proved that the Herald empennage was capable of withstanding by a wide margin the full range of loading which it would receive in service.

The twin-wheeled, tricycle undercarriage was a product of Electro-Hydraulics Ltd, which had been associated with Handley Page since the early days. It combined rigid structure and low pressure twin tyres. Comprehensive strength tests were carried out on detailed components as well as complete units.

The Herald went into service with a British Certificate of Airworthiness to the Transport Category (Passenger) standard with group A performance - the highest possible standard of airworthiness. There was little airline pilots could do to the aircraft that had not been covered during the rigorous and intensive testing programme. For example, on one day alone 176 stalls were performed.

Both engines were shut down many times to measure drag characteristics. To give just one example of the Herald exceeding its requirements; it could lose its electrical generators and still safely continue to any destination within 90min flying time.

Basic performance considerations

Handley Page was one of the first aircraft manufacturers to appreciate that with more stringent safety regulations coming into force – particularly in relation to performance after engine failure – airlines would soon find existing equipment unprofitable for themselves and unpopular with their passengers.

Thus Handley Page designers conceived the Herald as a fast, comfortable airliner incorporating fail-safe construction, long fatigue life, ease of maintenance and economy of operation – essential points in the make-up of a modern short-to-medium range airliner. Also purchase price had to be kept lower than contemporary contenders in the short-field class. (The Dart Herald was initially offered at £40,000 less than the Fokker Friendship, which was anticipated to catch a large chunk of the American market due the participation of Fairchild in the United States).

The flight testing programme for any civil airliner falls into three stages: the preliminary assessment of the aircraft's behaviour (occupying 50 to 100hr); the development of the aircraft and its equipment to the required airworthiness standards (this can take many hundreds of hours in the air); and proving the forecast economies of operation for route flying. The Herald came through all these with flying colours.

Any civil aircraft's flight manual must cover performance in both temperate and tropical climates. Thus the Herald was tested not only in England but also in Libya and Kenya. On tropical trials at Tripoli it met the unusual combination of high temperatures and sandy conditions, but proved equal to both. Most impressive, however, were the single-engined take-off trials at Nairobi airport. Here the Herald made dozens of short take-offs and landings to a pre-set pattern, each circuit being filmed by a Handley Page camera crew. The special test camera had been flown out from England in the Herald, together with a mountain of test equipment and spares – not to mention the trials team of pilots, technicians and engineers.

As well as these overseas trials, Herald sales tours were used to prove the aircraft (q.v.). Although little flight testing equipment could be carried on these intercontinental tours, the economics of operation were checked during actual route flying under airline procedures. Flight test technicians were present on every Herald demonstration tour to record aircraft performance and fuel consumption under all operating conditions.

Handling development

One of the most fascinating stages in development is reached when handling trials for stability, controllability, trim and stalling behaviour begin. These trials follow wind tunnel tests – which in the Herald's case were made at

Handley Page test plants at Radlett and Reading, and in the wind tunnels of the National Physical Laboratory and the Royal Aircraft Establishment.

Soon after the Herald prototype took to the air it became apparent that elevator power was inadequate when landing the aircraft at its forward centre of gravity limit. Various cures were tried. Firstly – as upward elevator setting range seemed reasonable – tailplane incidence was altered from zero to minus two degrees and various settings of the landing flaps tried. Results appeared satisfactory, although some trouble was experienced with the resultant lack of downward elevator movement in other flight conditions. The remedy was readily available, but when side slipping with the flaps at their landing setting and the engines at minimum power, the control column tended to 'snatch' forward.

From wind tunnel tests on powered models it was known that in level flight the tailplane carried a considerable download which balanced the nosedown pitching moment created by the flaps. This in turn was magnified by the slipstream blowing over the tailplane and flaps.

When the aircraft was side-slipped a further tailplane load distribution was introduced which contributed to a download on the tailplane root advancing into the side-slip. This load was too great for the aerofoil to carry, and airflow broke away from the elevator's lower surface. This sudden change in airflow resulted in elevator 'snatch', which tended to over-strain the control run.

With two problems to solve it was decided to return the tailplane to its original setting and to obtain the required elevator power for landing by increasing the size of the tailplane and elevator. The prototype tailplane was designed to minimise changes in longitudinal trim due to alterations in flap setting and engine power. With the introduction of the larger tailplane it was therefore necessary to modify the elevator balance system.

The developed elevator was balanced aerodynamically by the elliptical shape of its nose. Until larger, specially designed propellers became available, the prototype Dart Herald used ten-foot diameter propellers similar to those fitted to Viscounts. During development flying a loss in performance had been anticipated due to the low thrust of these propellers. At low airspeeds and high power settings pronounced elevator buffet was experienced, but in five months Handley Page flight test engineers overcame this and other problems, and succesfully developed the Herald into the most docile of medium-range airliners. When 12ft 6in diameter propellers became available there was an immediate reduction of buffet and an improvement in stability.

During the early flight testing of any prototype considerable aileron development is normally the rule. However, all that had been necessary since the Herald's first flight was a slight change of trim tab movement.

Stall and drag measurement

By careful design and thorough testing it is possible to design a twin-engined aircraft with a level of safety greater than its four-engined counterpart, together with a superior cruising performance at the same all-up weight. Many

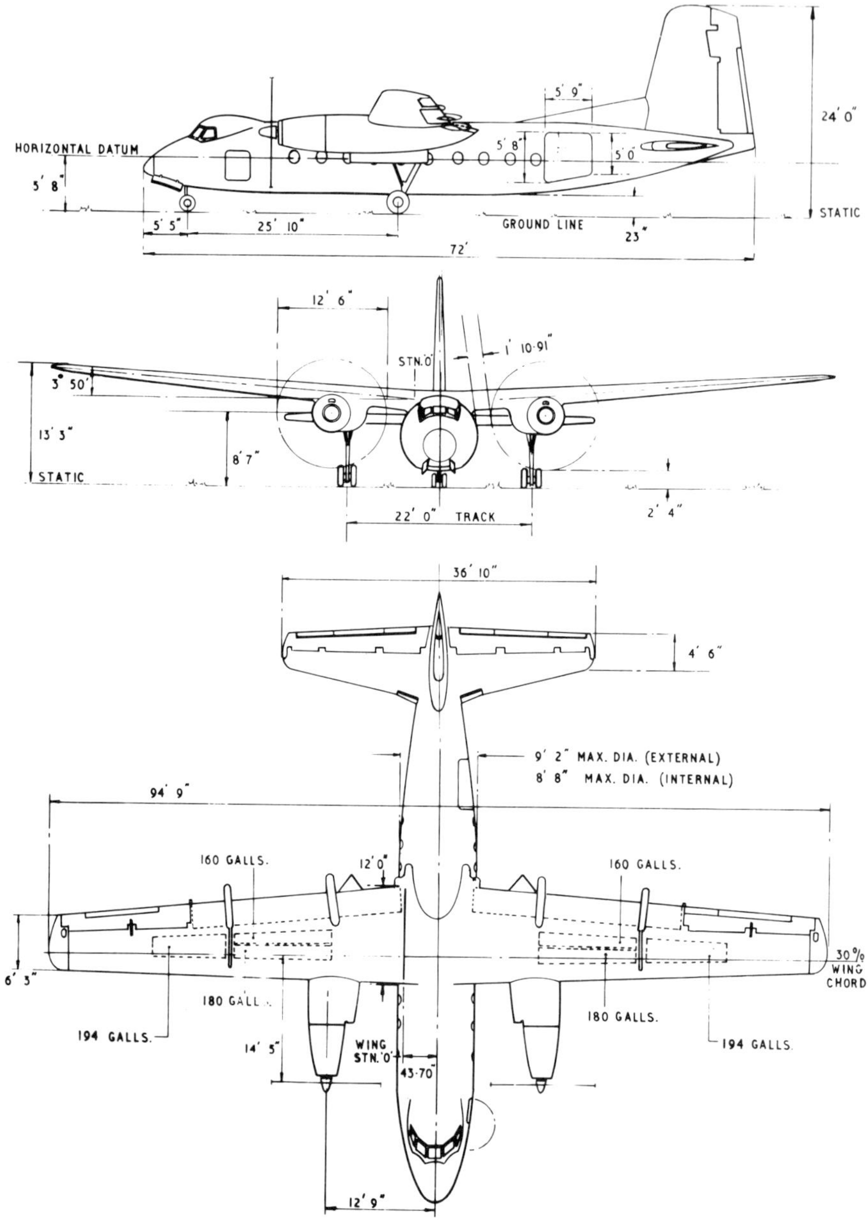

General arrangement of Dart Herald.

hundreds of measurements must be made in various climates to check an aircraft's estimated performance and to provide accurate charts for the flight and operations manuals. Isolating thrust or drag from flight test results is always complex, and because of this Handley Page decided to make direct measurements of the basic aircraft drag in symmetrical flight with various flap settings and over a wide range of speeds.

Aircraft drag in any given condition is calculated from the measured rate of descent with all engines inoperative. These tests were made with a Herald carrying a crew of five through smooth air in a clear sky. The aircraft was flown to 20,000ft and, with flaps and undercarriage retracted, both propellers were feathered. Rate of descent was timed and recorded, each run ending at 10,000ft, when the engines were restarted. Test descents were repeated until all combinations had been covered. Some 16 sets of results were measured and eventually it was possible to draw accurate drag curves, subsequently used to calculate all remaining performance results.

Another major parameter in flight testing is the behaviour and speed of the aircraft at the stall, since flight manual performance is based on these measurements. The Herald met all the stringent safety requirements with a good margin in hand.

Only during training is the airline pilot normally likely to approach stalling speed, when this phenomenon is shown to him in order to practise recovery. However, it is a common occurrence to the flight test crews when checking stall behaviour and speeds. As mentioned earlier, one crew managed 176 complete stalls in a single day. The aircraft was loaded to medium weight, with the c.g. at its forward limit, and a crew of three and 6,500lb of fuel were carried. At 12,000ft throttles were closed and six stalls made during the first descent.

Other conditions were also covered, such as the approach with power on. In turning flight the 'g' was increased until the aircraft stalled and rolled out of the turn. This established another safety feature - the Herald would not roll into the turn if a stall occurred.

Radiological crack detection

The disastrous effects of fatigue are countered in the Herald by 'fail-safe' construction. Fatigue cracks, when they occasionally occur after many thousands of hours of operation, cannot go beyond a certain limit, and when this pre-determined limit has been reached the cracks are repaired.

Comprehensive tests to destruction proved that the Herald's structure surpassed all safety requirements. By using radiological techniques, Herald operators did not need to strip their airliners, for the X-ray eye could see inside the structure without the need to dismantle the aircraft. The portable equipment was both quick to set up and simple to use. Basically, the three components which made up the apparatus were an X-ray tube, a control console and, with its mounting clamp, a sensitised plate on which the final image appeared. The X-ray tube was another item in the after-sales service evolved to keep the Heralds flying and profitable.

Dust bowl and mud bath trials

Unique trials in dust bowl and mud bath conditions were undertaken by a Herald to show the aircraft's suitability for operation from the roughest type of airstrip. Vegetation and top soil from a 2,000-yard strip were cleared from the sandy sub-soil of the RAF station at Martlesham Heath in Suffolk. This strip, after being deliberately cut up into deep longitudinal and cross-wise furrows until it looked like a battlefield, represented conditions far worse than anything normally expected.

So soft was the surface that no accurate bearing strength could be measured. In sun and heavy rain the fully-loaded Herald made extensive taxiing trials. It also repeatedly took off and landed in a 17kt cross-wind, using only 300 yards of runway. Ministry of Aviation officials and Army and RAF staff officers - particularly concerned with air transport problems - were present and saw the Herald, with its nose wheel completely immersed and one main wheel 18in deep in sand and mud, extricate itself using less than three-quarters of its own power and continue its taxiing under full control. A careful watch was kept for signs of damage or strain during these arduous trials. Propellers came out unscathed, and wheel bays were free from flying sand and mud. No fault of any description was found.

Ditching

To investigate the Herald's ditching behaviour, a 102in span dynamic model was tested in the fluid dynamics laboratories of Saunders-Roe. Touch-downs on surfaces varying from smooth to the equivalent of four-foot waves were filmed with a high-speed camera and analysed. At the same time, gauges and accelerometers built into the model measured pressures and accelerations. The results proved the Herald's natural hydrodynamic stability. Photographs taken during typical tests, one in smooth water conditions and the other in a heavy swell, illustrated well the gull-like ease with which a Herald would alight on water.

Certain features likely to affect ditching were represented at scale strength. Flaps and tailplane were designed to fail at prescribed pressures and moments, and did so in some cases without any untoward effects. The strength of the fuselage was represented at a joint just aft of the wing trailing edge, and this showed no signs of failure even under the most severe conditions. Even in the worst conditions, landing across a heavy swell - contrary to the prescribed method of ditching - the Herald model demonstrated the aircraft's built-in stability. Initially planing across the crests without any prominent change of attitude, it settled at about 15kt. On first impact the tailplane broke away to allow the model to plane freely and in a straight line.

So, to sum up; perhaps many of the Herald's virtues are due to Sqn Ldr Hazelden's help and advice on the basic design of the controls. The comparative speed at which the aeroplane was developed into a docile, viceless aircraft was doubtless largely due to the enthusiasm of the Reading team. The rigorous flight programme went on from dawn to dusk: only at night did the fitters and engineers have a chance to service and modify their charge.

On Tour

A series of extensive demonstration tours began in April 1959. Competition was building up, and Handley Page felt it was important to re-kindle the interest of operators if sales were to be maintained. 1959 saw G-AODF make three major sales tours to all parts of the world under all kinds of arduous conditions - one of the toughest proving programmes ever undertaken by a new airliner. G-AODF visited Brazilian jungles, the Australian outback, Pakistan mountains and New Zealand south lands.

Throughout these trips invaluable experience was notched up. The aircraft demonstrated a high degree of reliability, never once having to depart from its scheduled programmes - an amazing and praiseworthy feat for a new aircraft. More than 135,000 miles of hard demonstration flying were logged in only 26 weeks, and G-AODF visited 44 countries on five continents. During its 516 flying hours it carried 4,276 passengers, many airline officials and air force officers, and made 429 landings on concrete, tarmac and sand.

First sales tour - India and the Near East

Delta Foxtrot left Britain for India on April 10, arriving there four days later. It was demonstrated in Delhi on April 16 and 17, Srinagar April 19 and 20, Calcutta April 22, Jorhat April 25 and Bangalore May 1 before members of the Indian Government, the Indian Air Force, airline executives and engineers.

The most arduous flying on this tour was undertaken from small unprepared airstrips in the Himalayas. Typical of these was Leh, a sandy strip situated in a broad valley in the upper reaches of the Indus. Leh's airstrip, 11,00ft above sea level, runs steeply downwards at a rate of four feet in every 12 yards and terminates abruptly in a 500ft hill surmounted by a monastery. It is surrounded by mountains rising to 17,000ft above sea level and landings and take-offs are made downhill because of the mountainous nature of terrain beyond the strip's higher end.

During the Herald's demonstration circuits from Leh, a simulated one-engine failure on take-off was carried out - the highest ever successfully attempted by a twin-engined aircraft. Later the Herald demonstrated its suitability for military supply dropping. Flying from Jorhat, it showed its paces by dropping supplies - both with and without parachutes - into practice zones. After that the aircraft visited the Nage hills, where it dropped supplies, in very difficult terrain.

The Dart Herald then flew to Ceylon (now Sri Lanka) and appeared at airstrips on the east side of the island at Ampori and Battacoloa. Both were less than 3,000ft in length. G-AODF was next seen at Colombo on May 4 and 5, and then flew on to Pakistan for demonstrations at Karachi on May 7.

On its return flight, the aircraft was displayed on the ground and in the air at

Teheran (May 10 and 11), Ankara (May 14) and Athens (May 16), eventually arriving back in England on May 20. Flown by Sqn Ldr H. F. Hazelden, G-AODF had taken 14 members of Handley Page's staff on the 18,500-mile tour, which encompassed 35 airfields. Total flying time was 123hr 30min.

Second sales tour - South America

At the end of June the prototype was off once again, this time bound for South America, where it was seen by government officials, senior air force officers and airline staff. The 2,000-mile, 8¼hr flight across the South Atlantic was made by night. Leaving Blackbushe on June 26, the Herald flew to Dakar in French West Africa, where it was prepared for its crossing to Recife in Brazil. Two 330gal external pylon tanks, attached before leaving England, were the only non-standard equipment used for the crossing. They raised the Herald's maximum fuel capacity from 1090 to 1750gal, and its absolute duration at cruising speed to ten hours (or about 2,300 statute miles range). The tanks, one under each wing, gave the necessary range to cross the South Atlantic from Dakar to Recife. They were removed before the plane began its tour and refitted later for the return flight.

At the time there was a lack of regular meteorological data in the area, no ocean weather ships were stationed along the route, and the only airstrip available for an emergency landing on the ocean crossing was Fernando da Noronha, a group of islands about 300 miles from Recife. Nevertheless, no difficulties were encountered by Sqn Ldr Hazelden and his navigator, F. R. Gustin.

The aircraft gave its first demonstration at Georgetown, British Guiana, on July 6, four days after arriving on the continent. This was followed by demonstrations in Caracas, Venezuela on July 8, 9 and 10, and in Bogota, Colombia, on the 14th and 15th.

Quito, Ecuador, was the next port of call, where it was seen on July 18, afterwards appearing at Lima, Peru, on the 20th and 21st. From there its tour brought the Herald to Bolivia for demonstration flights at Cochabamba on July 24, 25 and 26. Continuing to Chile, *Delta Foxtrot* visited Santiago on the 30th and went on to Buenos Aires, Argentina, where it was seen on August 2 and 3.

The next demonstrations were in Montevideo, Uruguay, on August 6 and 7, and in Porto Alegre, Brazil, on the 9th and 10th. Staying in Brazil for the rest of the tour, the aircraft was shown at Sao Paulo on the 13th and in Rio de Janeiro on August 16, 17 and 18.

G-AODF arrived back in England ten days later. The eight-week trip had taken in ten countries and covered 32,000 miles. Total flying time was 163hr 45min with an amazing 202 landings - the highest by far of any Herald tour.

Meanwhile, the first production Dart Herald, G-APWA, had been completed and had begun flight trials. G-AODF came back to the UK just in time for a quick wash and brush-up before showing its paces at the 1959 SBAC show at Farnborough in September. After that it was off again, this time to Australasia.

Third sales tour - Australasia and the Far East

Handley Page planned to send two Dart Heralds on the massive promotional tour. Between them, G-AODF and G-APWA were to cover some 60,000 miles and give demonstrations in 11 countries - New Zealand, Australia, New Guinea, Borneo, the Philippines, the Federation of Malaya, Singapore, Indonesia, Vietnam, Thailand and Burma.

This brought to 40 the total of lands visited by the jet-prop airliner since the first sales tour in April 1959. By the end of that year Heralds were flying at a new approved all-up weight of 39,000lb. This increased payload by 25 per cent and lowered operating costs to 8.85d a short ton statute mile and 1.07d a passenger mile - a very economic performance.

G-AODF was the only aircraft to fly on the opening day of Rongatai, Wellington's new close-to-the-city airport. To build the magnificent aerodrome, millions of tons of earth, including a whole hill, were removed. On the big day - October 24, 1959 - there was a high wind and the weather was appalling.

Delta Foxtrot, in the event the only Herald sent, then began an extensive tour to Christchurch, Canberra, Melbourne, Sydney, Port Moresby, Lae, Manila, Jesselton, Singapore, Kuala Lumpur, Djakarta, Saigon, Bangkok and Rangoon. Its itinerary involved long sea crossings, including the 1,200-mile passage of the Tasman Sea, although this included a refuelling stop at Norfolk Island.

As well as airline chiefs and government officials, senior air force officers were among those who inspected this Herald. Leading the tour parties was Grp Capt A. F. Bandidt, Handley Page's representative in Australia, New Zealand and the Far East. Australian-born Grp Capt Bandidt spent some 13 years in the RAAF and RAF, and after his retirement from the latter in 1946 he had made the first post-war solo flight from England to Australia.

The Herald's captain was Sqn Ldr Hazelden, who had long experience as a test pilot, both in the RAF and with Handley Page. Holder of the DFC and Bar, he had completed two operational tours with Bomber Command and taken part in the first 1,000-bomber raids on Germany. A student on the first course of the Test Pilots School (later the Empire Test Pilots School) at Boscombe Down, he had been posted to heavy aircraft testing on completion of the course. Hazelden believes he was the first pilot to develop the technique of actually doing engine cuts on take-off.

He joined Handley Page in 1947, and within a few months became chief test pilot. He was later responsible for the flight testing of several of the firm's aircraft, including the Hastings, Hermes, Victor and, of course, the Herald.

Because of his superb airmanship during his development flying of the Herald he received his second commendation from the Sovereign for Valuable Service in the Air. Hazelden retired as chief test pilot in July 1965, although he stayed with the company on other duties until joining Autair in May 1967 as a pilot, flying Heralds and HS748s. When Court Line folded in 1974 he was 59, and, in his own words, 'getting on a bit', so he didn't think there was much chance of flying again. However, after a spell of various odd jobs, Capt 'Spud' Murphy of Air Anglia rang him up early in 1976, and offered him the position of chief pilot with the airline at Aberdeen, which Hazelden accepted.

Ground engineers accompanying G-AODF (G-APWA was intended to fly out and replace *Delta Foxtrot*, but was not ready in time) included those who had kept it flying ceaselessly on its two long tours of Asia and South America. They volunteered for the third tour so that their experience could be used to make sure it was a success. The tour began at Auckland on October 19, 1959, and ended at Rangoon on December 15.

Delta Foxtrot proved the solid and sturdy reliability of the Herald when flying in the worst possible circumstances in New Guinea, where rugged mountains covered in forbidding dense jungle are commonplace. At the request of airline men it was flown to the most difficult of the country's small grass airfields. There, despite high altitude and temperature and unhelpful local topography, the airliner demonstrated its ability to get a big load into a small, unsurfaced field without difficulty.

All the airfields chosen were over 5,000ft above sea level, one of them - Wabaga - being at 6,500ft. They had short, sloping runways between 3,800ft and 4,250ft in length, and two of them - Goroka and Mount Hagen - only up-hill landings and down-hill take-offs could be made - hardly plain sailing, even for the above-average pilot. In fact, at Wabaga, after a landing run of less than 500 yards, the Herald began to roll backwards, until Sqn Ldr Hazelden re-applied his brakes.

A jet-prop aeroplane had not been seen at any of these aerodromes before. As in many other places all over the world, the Herald was the first modern local service airliner to make an appearance there. During the demonstration, while flying at 12,500ft, a local pilot asked Hazelden to cut an engine, firmly believing that they would lose height. To his surprise the by no means lightly-loaded Herald rose another 500ft on the power of only one of its Darts.

After leaving New Guinea, G-AODF flew via North Borneo and Labuan to its next appointment - the Manila Air Week, an annual event for the air-minded Filipinos. During the international air display which highlighted these celebrations the Herald, in competition with many of the world's finest air force demonstration teams, became the star of the show. Its spectacular performance gained spontaneous applause from an appreciative crowd.

From the Philippines the Herald flew to Singapore, Malaya, Indonesia, Vietnam and Burma, where it was seen by air forces and airlines intent on modernising their short-haul networks. It arrived back at Woodley on December 18, after a total flying time of 229hr 15min. *Delta Foxtrot* made 137 landings and visited 49 airfields on this tour.

Fourth sales tour - West Africa and South America

The first production aircraft, G-APWA, left England shortly after dawn on March 16, 1960, to start the fourth Herald demonstration and sales tour. *En route* to Latin America, *Whisky Alpha* first flew to Ghana and Nigeria. In both of these countries the national airlines used DC-3s, and Handley Page wanted to show them the Herald's suitability as a replacement for their piston-engined Daks.

In order to emphasise the point, G-APWA was flown into Kumasi, one of Ghana's most difficult airfields. No problems were encountered, even though the starboard engine was feathered on take-off, as it was a few days later, when the aeroplane visited Jos, considered to be one of Nigeria's worst airstrips.

Returning northwards to Dakar, *Whisky Alpha* opened the second phase of its tour by making the third crossing of the South Atlantic by a Herald. Its arrival at Recife in Brazil coincided with calls for help from flood victims at Fortaleza, where torrential rains had caused a dam to burst. The Herald's crew immediately flew the 800 miles to the stricken area with 5,500lb of urgently-needed clothing and medical supplies before setting out the following day for Rio de Janeiro to begin demonstrations to South American airlines.

During the following seven weeks G-APWA visited 44 airports and airstrips in Brazil, Argentina and Uruguay. At more than one-third of the 25 strips visited in Brazil it was the first prop-jet aircraft seen locally. Airline pilots were given the chance to fly the aircraft themselves and, as was usual on these tours, G-APWA visited airfields which airlines considered would provide the toughest test of short-field performance. Typical of these was Lajes, in Brazil, a 1,000-yard strip composed of mud and stones 3,000ft above sea level. Here the Herald impressed its complement of air force officers by stopping in under 500 yards and getting airborne, weighing 35,370lb, in little more than half the

G-APWA (c/n 149) - Whisky Alpha - in BEA colours early on in its highly adventurous career. Note the long-range tank under the wing.

length of the strip.

G-APWA visited many other marginal strips in Brazil, the shortest of which had an effective length of only 800 yards. It often averaged 7½hr flying every day. Much good-natured comment was caused by the frequent sight of the fully-loaded Herald whining contemptuously over the top of Rio's Sugarloaf mountain – a feat accomplished only once before, and then by a lightly-laden aircraft. It usually cleared the 1,430ft high summit, situated only two and a quarter miles from the end of the Santos Dumont runway, by at least 500ft, while other aircraft turned aside to fly down the neighbouring valley or out to sea.

Continuing its tour in the Argentine, the Herald once again visited the country's worst airfields with the pilots, operating staff and managements of six airlines.

The return to England, which included the fourth crossing of the Atlantic by a Herald, was made by way of Dakar and Gibraltar. Such was the interest in the Argentine that, shortly after its return, *Whisky Alpha* flew over to Holland and carried President Arturo Frondizi of the Argentine to Gatwick for his official visit to Great Britain. Total flying time on the tour was 217hr 45min. *Whisky Alpha* had made 158 landings and consumed 36,267gal of fuel at an average rate of consumption of 168gal per hour.

A king takes control

In December 1959 King Hussein of Jordan took the controls of G-APWA during a demonstration flight, and carried out an appraisal of the aircraft's flying qualities for nearly an hour. The King, an accomplished pilot, was keen to gain first-hand experience of the Herald, which had potential civil and military transport applications in countries such as his. He was accompanied by Wg Cdr 'Jock' Dalgleish, officer commanding the Royal Jordanian Air Force, and Mr John Allam, Handley Page's deputy chief test pilot, who captained the aircraft during the flight.

All aspects of handling performance were closely examined, including single-engined flying. This entailed cutting one engine straight after one of the take-offs; the aircraft continued its climb effortlessly on half its total power.

Before joining Handley Page, Flt Lt Allam (not to be confused with the company's chief designer, John Allan) had served for 11 years in the RAF, completing 3,500hr on more than 60 types of aircraft, thereby gaining extensive experience as a test pilot.

When he joined Handley Page in August 1954, Allam was engaged on testing the Victor jet bomber, and he took the Herald's formidable stable-mate through the sound barrier in 1957. He also made the maiden flight of the prototype Victor B2 – over half as powerful again as its predecessor – on February 20, 1959.

Allam flew Dart Heralds for many hours, and was responsible for the first flight of the Series 200. It was largely due to his vast test flying experience in general, and his fine appreciation of the Herald in particular, that a full

Certificate of Airworthiness was obtained so quickly for this larger Herald.

From 1960 onwards *Whisky Alpha* was put to work showing its abilities all over the world, from Brazil to Sweden and from South Africa to Saudi Arabia, in addition to numerous demonstrations in England before visiting air force and airline officials.

In July 1960, after the demanding South American tour, Air Cdre I. G. Esplin, director of operational requirements at the Air Ministry, flew in the Herald. The Air Ministry was interested in the type because of its wide military appeal, as well as its potential as a flying classroom for radar calibration. The Royal Australian Air Force expressed interest in the Herald as possible new equipment for its Transport Command, and *Whisky Alpha* was also shown to the RAF at Transport Command HQ, Upavon.

In August that year the Handley Page agents in Austria, the Kraftl company, said arrangements were nearing completion for an initial sale of two Dart Heralds to the Austrian Government despite intense competition. The cost would have been £400,000, and the aircraft would have been operated by a new company set up to administer domestic services in conjunction with Austrian Airlines.

In February 1961 *Whisky Alpha* was demonstrated to a Venezuelan business delegation and in April to Cambrian Airways (q.v.) Later that month it flew to Sweden to show its paces in front of Swedish Air Force top brass. Also in 1961 BOAC chairman Sir Matthew Slattery met Handley Page executives to discuss the need of some of the corporation's associated companies for a DC-3 replacement. BOAC had shareholdings in British West Indian Airways, Gulf Aviation and Aden Airways, all of which operated short- to medium-length routes.

In November 1963 *Whisky Alpha* was demonstrated in South Africa and Rhodesia before going on lease to Sadia as PP-ASV early in the next year.

Demonstration tour of Southern Europe, the Near East and East Africa

In early November 1961 Dart Herald G-ARTC (formerly G-AODF), resplendent in Maritime Central Airways' livery, left England on a five-week demonstration tour involving many thousands of miles of flying in Southern Europe, the Near East and East Africa. Up to that time, more than a staggering 200,000 miles of 'see-it-in-action' touring had been flown by Heralds in 60 countries.

In Italy, the first country on the itinerary, the 56-seat Herald made a series of proving flights on behalf of Itavia, which had ordered two Herald Series 200s at the Farnborough air show in September 1961. When the contract was signed, Itavia had only been operating services for three years. The airline was able to make a close study of the aircraft on their routes during the Herald's three-day visit to Italy, which began with flights from Ciampino (Rome) airport. Top airline officials were greatly impressed with the aeroplane's STOL capabilities. Thereafter, the Herald carried out proving flights from Rome to Ancona and

Taranto. Wherever it went in Italy, it attracted crowds of admirers.

Throughout this tour, numerous demonstrations - many on an *ad hoc* basis - were given to airlines operating difficult routes. Flights with full payload were the order of the day, and the airliner returned at the end of the tour having met every flight schedule. It had visited nearly two dozen airfields in very hot climates, often flying specimen routes between several of them. The chiefs of several airlines which examined and flew the Herald had previously been unable to find a short- to medium-range turboprop aircraft that suited their needs or could operate in their climates with a profitable payload. With its tropical testing satisfactorily completed, the Herald fulfilled such stringent demands, its makers claimed.

Demonstration visit to Saudi Arabia

In 1962 G-APWA flew to Saudi Arabia, furnished with its special VIP interior used by Prince Philip on his South American tour (q.v.). The country was one of the few which had not previously seen the Dart Herald on a demonstration visit. The aircraft touched down on planned arrival time after a three-hour flight from Amman, Jordan, piloted by Capt L. Matthey, a British United Airways training captain. Awaiting *Whisky Alpha* at Jedda airport were local dignitaries, Saudi Arabian Airlines executives, and government officials, who bombarded the crew with all types of technical questions.

Among guests who flew on a demonstration flight were pilots of Saudi Arabian Airlines. After flying on one engine to show the Herald's good performance, speed was reduced when both engines were operating normally to demonstrate the lateral stability of the aircraft near the stall. With passengers on board, a stall could not be effected. This is one of the most fascinating Herald manœuvres. With the control column held back, the wings remain completely level while the nose pitches gently up and down like a porpoise.

During their hundred of thousands of miles of demonstration flying Heralds were conspicuous for their outstanding performance in the air and their remarkable serviceability. Progress was never held up by a lack of spares. In fact, only once was a part needed which was not carried aboard the aircraft. This, a generator, was sent out immediately to meet the Herald at its next staging point.

During the many months of intensive touring, it was only twice necessary to delay a demonstration because of unserviceability. A faulty micro-switch caused one delay at Port Moresby, and in Ceylon a burst tyre kept passengers waiting for 45min. A Herald departed from its pre-planned schedule only once, and this was thought to be due to local fuel. With these three exceptions, Heralds performed with clockwork regularity. This must surely be due to the fact that, when the tours were planned, it was decided that the aircraft would operate as self-contained units, carrying their own ground crew, servicing equipment and spares.

The ground crew of three men with a service engineer in charge maintained the aircraft throughout their tours. In addition, there were also two inspectors.

This team carried out the normal daily maintenance and routine inspections Check 1 and 2. It also removed and fitted the long-range under-wing tanks for the Atlantic crossings.

Usually all work was done in the open, with the Darts being started on internal batteries. During one week in India a Herald confined its operations to aerodromes with no ground starting facilities at all. The ground servicing equipment comprised a jacking frame and a jack for tyre changes and brake maintenance, a lightweight towing bar (seldom used because of the Herald's ability to manœvre in confined spaces due to its 50° nosewheel steering lock) and two commercial aluminium ladders. Cradles on which to store the long-range tanks and propeller flight tool kits were also carried.

Routine daily maintenance was usually all that was needed to keep the Heralds flying, their wonders to perform. One morning in New Zealand the ground crew had a rather unusual job to tackle – removing a nest in the tail fin built overnight by an enterprising bird!

Praise was certainly lavished on the sturdy little aircraft. Unfortunately, only a few of those who offered kind remarks actually bought it in the years to come. Mr Robert McKean, BEA's Scottish manager, said that with a half a century of aircraft construction behind them it was no surprise Handley Page had produced, in the Dart Herald, 'what may well be the ideal short- and medium-range airliner'.

Here are some other quotes: Air Cdre M. A. Rahman, Chief of air staff, Pakistan Air Force: 'I consider the Herald an ideal replacement for the Dakota operating in both the military and civil role'.

Mr Aristotle Onassis, chairman, Olympic Airways: 'The Herald is the finest aircraft in its class'.

Gen F. A. Correa de Mello, Brazilian Air Minister: 'It is an excellent aircraft in its class for rapid transportation from normal C-47 airstrips'.

Maj Seidl, COMTA, Brazilian Air Force: 'The Herald is the best aircraft of its type we have had to handle. No Brazilian airfield could present difficulty to the Herald'.

Mr Hussein Bey, technical director, Turkish Airlines: 'The Herald's robust structure and accessibility for maintenance are outstanding'.

Mr Green, director of civil aviation, New Guinea: 'The Herald was the first turboprop to fly into New Guinea's outback strips. Its performance was very impressive'.

The Hon H. G. Townley, MP, Australian Minister of Defence: 'I have enjoyed flying the Herald. It is a well made, high performance aircraft especially suited to the RAAF's type of operation'.

Royal Tour by Dart Herald

News that HRH Prince Philip had chosen the Dart Herald for his 11-country tour of South America in early 1962 came as a tremendous boost to Handley Page. The choice of aircraft for this, the longest royal tour by air up to that time, was naturally of great importance, as many places to be visited had primitive airfields. BEA, who had to provide the aircraft, chose the Herald for its STOL capabilities, minimum servicing requirements, reliability and toughness.

Under the command of BEA's flight training manager Capt 'Bill' Johnson, two complete crews were selected and prepared for the three months away. With them was Mr G. McCrea from Handley Page's servicing department.

The Herald was, of course, no stranger to South America, having twice before demonstrated its go-anywhere capabilities on that continent. In Bolivia, for example, a Dart Herald flew from La Paz, the world's highest airfield, with a full complement of passengers while only using one engine, demonstrating its great power reserve and safety.

On January 11, 1962, G-APWC left Heathrow on its 7,000-mile ferry flight to the West Indies, piloted by Sqn Ldr Hazelden. For this long journey two 330gal pylon fuel tanks were fitted, adding another 660gal to the Herald's normal 1,080gal capacity. The 1,740gal gave it about ten hours flying duration.

Five days later Hazelden handed the plane over to Capt Johnson and his crew, and the next morning route proving began. *Whisky Charlie* was fitted out as a 44-seater to carry the royal entourage. During this time the Handley Page demonstrator, G-APWA, which had been specially prepared as Prince Philip's personal aircraft with a 21-seat executive layout, had been flown out by Capt Dennis Warren of BEA in readiness for his arrival. It flew a similar route to that taken by *Whisky Charlie* (Las Palmas, Dakar and then across the South Atlantic to Brazil).

The first leg of the royal tour started on February 9 from Mackenzie airport, British Guiana. The itinerary took the two Heralds along the west coast through Venezuela to Colombia, Equador, Peru, Bolivia and Chile, then across the Andes to Argentina, Paraguay, Uruguay, and northward to Brazil before returning to Argentina.

On the return journey the Heralds flew the length of Brazil back to British Guiana, then by way of the West Indies to British Honduras and to Grand Cayman Island, from where Prince Philip flew back to London.

During the tour *Whisky Alpha* flew 34 out of 55 days over 62 sectors in a total flying time of 126hr 46min. Prince Philip flew on 49 of these sectors (he was an experienced Herald pilot, having been introduced to the aircraft by Hazelden), and was at the controls for 99 out of the 112 hours he spent on board.

Whisky Alpha's greatest flying time in one day was logged on April 1, when it covered 2,011 miles from Salvador (Brazil) to Mackenzie (British Guiana) in

10hr 28min. In contrast, the shortest flight was one of 11min, from one Lima airport to another.

As the royal Herald maintained its rigid schedule, its sister-ship kept in close attendance, occasionally leap-frogging with its important cargo of baggage. The mechanical reliability of both aircraft is shown in their superb adherence to schedule. Among the more remote landing grounds used was an Argentine ranch, where cattle had to be rounded up to clear a strip for Prince Philip to land.

Throughout the entire operation the two aeroplanes logged 471 flying hours and flew 100,000 miles, including the outward and return ferry flights and the initial proving flight. Check 1s were carried out on both Heralds at Santiago by BEA engineers aided by Mr McCrea. During the three months that the Heralds were abroad there were only two delays, one caused by a sudden change in the weather at Cordoba, where a heavy thunderstorm grounded the aircraft for four hours, and the other by a minor fault to an electrical indicator in the cockpit.

This latter problem was referred to by Prince Philip in a telegram sent to Sir Frederick Handley Page on his return; it read: 'I am sure you will be delighted to hear that the two Heralds gave excellent service throughout my tour of South America. I flew G-APWA for 99 hours and enjoyed every one of them. I am only sorry that the one minor mishap should have caused so much comment'.

At the end of the tour at Grand Cayman on April 5, the long-range underwing fuel tanks were once more fitted to the Heralds prior to the departure for Port of Spain. The two aircraft returned to London via Antigua,

Telegram from Prince Philip to "HP" after the Duke's grand tour of South America in Whisky Alpha.

Charges to pay ___s.4___d. RECEIVED

POST OFFICE
TELEGRAM

No.___ OFFICE STAMP
EDGWARE -7 APR.62 MIDDX.

Prefix. Time handed in. Office of Origin and Service Instructions. Words.

At___ ___m 77

At___m To___ By___

From___ By___ 108 2 11.5 WINDSOR CASTLE OHMS 60

SIR FREDERICK HANDLEY-PAGE CBE LIMES HOUSE STANMORE MIDDLES EX =

I AM SURE YOU WILL BE DELIGHTED TO HEAR THAT THE TWO HERALDS GAVE EXCELLENT SERVICE THROUGHOUT MY TOUR OF SOUTH AMERICA STOP I FLEW GAPWA FOR 99 HOURS AND ENJOYED EVERY ONE OF THEM STOP I AM ONLY SORRY THAT THE ONE MINOR MISHAP SHOULD HAVE CAUSED SO MUCH COMMENT =

PHILIP + 99 + ✝ TS 0

...e " TELEGRAMS ENQUIRY" or call, with this form ...accompanied by this form, and, if possible, the envelope. B or C

G-APWA (c/n 149) was converted into a sumptuous 21-seat executive layout for Prince Philip for his South American tour in 1962. (Handley Page)

Bermuda, Gander and Keflavik.

In spite of meeting unexpected weather conditions halfway across the Atlantic, which caused exceptional icing, the two airliners were able to continue their homeward journey to Renfrew in fine fettle. When they arrived at Heathrow on April 14 the crews were welcomed home by Mr Anthony Milward, BEA's chief executive.

The idea of converting the Herald to a VIP or executive fit was borne in mind when the design was drawn up. From the flight deck to the tail bulkhead, the cabin has an uninterrupted length which lends itself to various interior arrangements.

That chosen for Prince Philip's aircraft had a private cabin in the rear fuselage, furnished on the port side with facing armchairs. Between them was a polished table, the sides of which folded upwards to make a rest-stand for books. A plinth at the side housed an interphone, and on the opposite side of the cabin was a long settee which converted into a rest couch. The fore and aft partitions were in Pettigo Harvest Beige and Nassau, with curtains in brown and green with gold lurex thread. The toilet was in the tail section, with a hold for luggage beyond. Because the Herald's cabin floor is so close to the ground, passenger steps were small enough to be carried.

The staff cabin in the centre of the fuselage was arranged with seats for 14 people in a conventional layout, but with a greater than normal pitch. Apart from window and partition curtains in yellow and neutral, the colour scheme was similar to the private cabin. In the front fuselage was a second toilet, and, on the other side of a central gangway, a curtained baggage compartment. To enable full course meals to be served, a comprehensive galley unit with ice box was installed aft of the flight deck bulkhead.

The port side of the front fuselage housed a standard Herald radio rack, containing dual VHF communication, single VHF navigation, HF communication, dual ADF navigation, intercommunication and public address system equipment. The flight deck installation was standard, with the exception of Bendix weather radar, the scanner for which was fitted in an extended nose cap similar to those fitted to Heralds then operating with Nordair of Canada. Some idea of the speed at which the conversions were carried out can be gauged from the fact that G-APWA was delivered for service, complete in BEA colours, in December 1961, less than two months after the order for it to be made ready was first received.

In service - UK and Channel Islands operators

BRITISH EUROPEAN AIRWAYS

The first (and only) three production Dart Herald Series 100s (G-APWB-D) were ordered by the Ministry of Supply in June 1959 for evaluation by BEA on their Scottish 'Highlands and Islands' services. They were laid down in 1959 and built by Handley Page at Woodley, Reading. The 44-seat aircraft were scheduled for delivery to BEA in January and February 1961, but did not in fact arrive until 1962, when they were put into service under a leasing arrangement with the Ministry of Aviation. Cut-off date was October 31, 1966.

Following improvements at Scottish airports Viscounts replaced the Heralds, which had served the Scottish islands from Glasgow, Edinburgh, Aberdeen and Inverness for four years. They had flown from some of Britain's shortest airline landing fields in some of Britain's most notoriously tricky weather. Heralds helped maintain the tradition of public service established on these routes since before the war.

G-APWB was first painted in Jersey Airlines' colour scheme and leased from

Passengers embark in Series 100 Herald G-APWD (c/n 152) at Kirkwall airport, Orkney. (BEA)

Handley Page with demonstrator G-APWA pending delivery of Jersey's own Series 201s. It went to BEA on March 10, 1962. First to be delivered was G-APWC on January 5, 1962, even though the grass airfield at Woodley had an eight-inch layer of snow. Take-off weight was 32,200lb.

Whisky Charlie was fitted with long range tanks on underwing pylons for transatlantic flight, and departed for Jamaica on January 11 that year. Together with *Whisky Alpha* it was used on the Duke of Edinburgh's South American tour, which took in 11 countries between February and April 1962. It returned to BEA on May 18.

The third BEA machine, G-APWD, was delivered on April 30, 1962. Although G-AODF and G-APWA were not owned by BEA, they flew in the company's livery at one stage.

The Government had ordered the Heralds to help Handley Page lay down a production line and boost the programme in order to compete with the Fokker Friendship in the export market.

In December 1959 G-APWA arrived in Scotland wearing BEA's newly-introduced colour scheme of red, black and white, to carry out proving trials in anticipation of the 1961 summer services when Heralds were to take over from the DC-3s.

Captained by John Allam, Handley Page's deputy chief test pilot, *Whisky Alpha* touched down in blustery weather at Renfrew. On leaving Renfrew for the first of the proving and demonstration flights to Islay and Campbeltown, the aeroplane was airborne within 15sec with 44 aboard. This was the first time these places had seen a turboprop civil aircraft, and great interest was shown by local dignitaries and the general public alike. Next day G-APWA, carrying 40 passengers, took off from Renfrew for Sumburgh in the Shetland Islands; it then flew on to Kirkwall, Grimsetter, Aberdeen, Inverness and Edinburgh. In four days of proving and demonstrating, the Herald carried out 11 take-offs and landings.

The 'Highlands and Islands' services never made money - they were primarily run as a social service. All maintenance work was done at night and on Sundays, because the Heralds were kept flying all day for six days a week. There was no reserve aircraft because of a deliberate policy of keeping costs to a minimum. Average aircraft utilisation was 1,500hr per year.

The Herald was well-liked by ground crew and much freight was flown on these trips. After the introduction of TV to the Orkneys, 8,000 sets were flown there from Aberdeen. Freight varied widely from parcels and mail to bulky items such as gas stoves, live lobsters, day-old chicks and machine tools.

In 1964 the average aircraft utilisation was over 1,500hr per hear, with a mean sector time of only 35min. In the 1964/65 financial year BEA recorded an average passenger load factor of 64 per cent on the three aircraft, achieved 4,364 revenue flying hours and carried 113,200 passengers. By March 1965 they had together carried more than 280,300 passengers and 1,650 tons of cargo. G-APWB had logged the highest number of hours for any Herald - 5,050 - by April 30, 1965, and the second highest total of landings - 8,858.

JERSEY AIRLINES

The highlight of the third day of the SBAC air show at Farnborough in September 1960 was the news that six Handley Page Dart Heralds had been ordered by Jersey Airlines for operation on their scheduled routes from the Channel Islands. The airline had the distinction of being the first commercial buyer in the world to order the Dart Herald. Deliveries were planned to start in June 1961, but in the event Handley Page chartered Heralds to the airline before Jersey Airlines' first Herald, G-APWE, was delivered on January 4, 1962.

Jersey Airlines ordered the 48-50 seat version (the Series 200), incorporating the 42in extension to the fuselage. Announcing the signing of the £1,500,000 contract, chairman and managing director Mr M. L. Thomas said that his company had closely evaluated all prop-jet aircraft in the short-haul class.

'None showed such a high profit potential as the Herald over our short-stage lengths', he said. These average only 100 nautical miles. I have been particularly impressed by the proving of the Herald on the most difficult air routes of more than 50 countries. Their servicing record on these trips has been remarkable.'

As far back as October 12, 1956, the four-engined Herald prototype had visited the Channel Islands for Jersey Airlines to evaluate. Its STOL capability was well demonstrated at Alderney, the smallest of the Channel Islands to have an aerodrome. Its grass airstrip – which also served as a cow pasture – was only 960 yards long, and beyond it lay high cliffs and the sea. From Hurn airport Herald G-AODF flew with its 19 passengers to Alderney in 34min. Prior to its arrival, cattle grazing on the landing strip were driven to one side, bridled and tethered. The plane was then cleared to land.

Conditions were not good, the island being surrounded by cloud which came down to within 100ft of the aerodrome. Visibility was less than half a mile, and no radio aids were available. Despite this a successful approach was made, and the aircraft came to rest after a ground run of only 400 yards across the wet grass. It was the largest-ever aircraft to land at Alderney. The G-AODF then flew on to Guernsey, later returning to its home airfield at Woodley via Hurn.

At this time the appearance of the Fokker Friendship cut the ground from under the original piston-engined Herald. Eighteen months went by as the type was re-engined with Darts. Then, on April 1, 1958, the prorotype Dart Herald came to Jersey for a demonstration. Jersey Airlines may have preferred its Dutch competitor, but the heavy import duty on foreign aircraft made the Herald far cheaper. Another important factor was seating. Mr Thomas said that the 42 extra inches of his Series 200 aircraft, compared with the Series 100, would be used to accommodate six more passenger seats. The Friendship was only a 44-seater.

'During the peak holiday season of July and August alone', he said, 'each Jersey Airlines Herald will make 600 flights. If the extra passengers pay an average fare of £3, each seat will earn £1,800. During these two months, 21,600 more passengers will be carried; this will give additional revenue of £64,800 for

G-APWA proudly displays the flags of countries visited on its nose. Jersey May 17, 1961.
(Flight International)

the six aircraft.'

The Handley Page demonstrator G-APWA arrived on May 17, 1961, and began services the same day. The aircraft was chartered to the airline to allow it to gain early passenger-carrying experience with the new type. Shortly after, it was followed by another on charter (G-APWB, the first to be painted in Jersey Airlines colours), and the two Series 100 Heralds were to bear the brunt of the summer season traffic on the airline's busiest route.

A third chartered Herald, G-APWC (with G-APWA) made an extensive tour of South America in 1962 with HRH the Duke of Edinburgh. The crew for the VIP visit was provided by BEA, and included Capt S. J. Nicolle from Jersey. There was some talk of Jersey Airlines providing the crew. *Whisky Alpha* had a red cheat line and rudder with 'Jersey Airlines' titling above the cheat line between the wing leading edge and cockpit windows.

On the heavy London service in the summer of 1961, the Heralds were flying five return trips starting from Gatwick at 8.10 a.m., with the last flight leaving Jersey at 7.30 in the evening. The Herald service provided 500 seats compared with 320 seats available on the DC-3s.

Although the aircraft was designed for short to medium ranges, the airline also successfully operated them on ultra-short sectors when the weight of traffic demanded the larger capacity. An example of this was the Jersey-Dinard run – a distance of 38 miles.

If ever a new aircraft was put into passenger-carrying service 'at the deep end', it was the Herald on Jersey Airlines' routes. During the peak season, from June until October, the operator's high-density services flew hundreds of holiday-makers daily between the islands and the mainlands of Britain, Ireland and the Continent. Between them the two Heralds shared the bulk of traffic on the Gatwick-Jersey and Bournemouth-Jersey routes in 1961, logging 20 trips per day. As expected, a very high record of serviceability was achieved.

Load factors on the Jersey routes were high. On the Bournemouth run the average figure was 85 per cent, while on Saturdays it reached 95 per cent. Corresponding load factors on the London route were 78 per cent and 87 per cent respectively. Altogether each of the two 44-seat Heralds carried an average of 36,883 passengers during 960 flights in their first four months of service.

In the 1962 summer season, four Series 200 Heralds flew eight direct daily services. *Whisky Echo* arrived in January that year, and by May 22 G-APWF and 'WG had been delivered, with *Whisky Hotel* following on June 6. The Civil Air Ensign was painted on the tail of these aircraft.

Jersey was served from London, Bournemouth, Glasgow, Manchester, Exeter and Paris; Guernsey from London and Bournemouth. From early June

G-APWE (c/n 153) in its original Jersey Airlines livery in 1961. This aircraft still flies with Air UK.(BUA)

until the end of September the Herald fleet was scheduled to fly a total of 2,945 hours. Each airliner operated seven hours a day, making ten landings every day throughout the season; during the normal hours of service each Herald touched down, on average, every 50min.

At the end of October, Jersey Airlines reverted to its off-season schedules. To attract the hard-core of business travellers between the Channel Islands and London, the Herald introduced a new luxury executive flight. With a connecting rail service at Gatwick, it provided a fast terminal-to-terminal run between Jersey and London. Equipped with bar and refreshment facilities, it proved so popular with the 'regulars' that there were requests for season tickets.

During the summer of 1962 the entire fleet was deployed on Saturdays, Sundays, Wednesdays and Fridays, while one aircraft was withdrawn from service on the remaining days. This left little room in the schedules for a reserve aircraft.

• • •

1962 was the last year of independent operations by Jersey Airlines aircraft. On May 20 that year the airline was acquired by Air Holdings Ltd, who later reorganised all of the airlines in the Air Holdings group. So was born BU (Channel Islands) Airways on November 1, 1962, which became responsible for the operation of most of the scheduled passenger and cargo services to the Channel Islands and Isle of Man using Dakotas and Heralds.

BU(CI)A came into operation on January 1, 1963, by merging the routes of Jersey Airlines with the north of England network of Silver City Airways. In 1963 two more Heralds (G-APWI and WJ), the last to be painted in the Jersey Airlines grey-blue-white-gold colours, arrived. They were formally handed over to Capt Bernard Gardiner, director of operations, but were the property of Transair, and left the Handley Page works with the BU insignia on the side. The Jersey Airlines Heralds were gradually repainted in BU titling after August 1, 1963.

The Jersey Airlines name was such a good advertisement that it was kept and used all through the 1962 and '63 seasons. The Heralds in the old livery began operating on the longer routes, such as Jersey-Blackpool-Isle of Man, but this met with strong protests from the Manxmen. Many northern people who traditionally took their holiday on the Isle of Man had begun instead to fly to Jersey, and that just wasn't playing the game! So the Jersey Airlines livery was dropped for the more anonymous BU(CI)A.

In March 1962 the chief company in the British United group, British United Airways, ordered a seventh Herald for VIP use, based at Gatwick. It was delivered in November that year. From April 1963 to April 1965, the six Heralds carried more than 366,700 passengers and flew some two and a half million miles. Average sector length was 170 miles.

In April 1965, when a Jersey-based Herald made its home base at Blackpool, it represented a great victory for local operations staff. For a long time they had

G-APWG (c/n 155) in the attractive British United livery. (Handley Page)

wanted to see a modern turbine-powered aircraft serving BU's northern customers, but for a couple of seasons past they had to contend with the now-you-see-it, now-you-don't benefit of partial Herald services. This was because the timings of seasonal flying did not leave enough hours to spare to keep one of the smart blue-red-yellow liveried Heralds up north.

The Heralds achieved between 40 and 50hr utilisation a week. The popular Blackpool-Isle of Man 30min run calls for a special kind of non-existent short hop aircraft, 'a 100-seat fixed-wheel aircraft that can be parked and forgotten all winter', as BUA northern sales superintendent Mr Brian Bradley described it. For 100,000 people a year were flying on this highly seasonal route.

In November 1966 BUA introduced their new colour scheme of a sand and blue stripe, and for the 1967 season BU(CI)A acquired two more Heralds; G-ASKK from BMA, who ran it regularly to Jersey and who obtained a BUA Viscount in exchange; and G-AVEZ, formerly Globe Air's HB-AAH.

From January 1, 1968, BU(CI)A began operating independently from British United to try and put the airline's Channel Islands services on a money-making basis. General manager Capt G. Thomas wrote the following in a letter to his staff: 'In recent years the group policy was that BUA and BU(CI)A should work on an integrated basis, but we recommended to the board that we

G-APWF (c/n 154) in British United Island Airways colours. Note addition of the "I". (BUA)

be left to work on our own.'

The airline was told by the directors of the Air Holdings Group that it must show the success of the new policy by April 1, 1968, as well as a stated profit by September 30.

Said Capt Thomas: 'For the past two or three years we have relied on BUA for a lot of services, like collecting revenue, and it has not worked out in every case. Here in the Channel Islands we are doing a completely different kind of work to that done by the long-distance airlines. We want to make air travel more off the peg, and we do not want to go on asking for fare increases'.

In effect, the new policy was a 're-separation' of the Jersey-based company. So in 1968 the airline, with Manx Airlines and Morton Air Services, left the Air Holdings group together with BUA and became a subsidiary of BUA (Holdings) Ltd. Later the same year British United Island Airways (BUIA) was formed by the grouping of BU(CI)A, BU(Manx)A and Mortons. By the end of 1969 BUA's sand and blue livery had altered slightly by the addition of an 'I' on the nose and tail logo to signify BUIA.

AUTAIR INTERNATIONAL AIRWAYS

Autair, the Court Line subsidiary, bought from the MOA in 1966 the three Herald Series 101s which BEA had had on lease and operated on their Scottish routes. They were acquired to help expand Autair's domestic scheduled services.

Three years earlier, two Heralds had been leased to Autair from Handley Page. G-ASKK was operated from August to December 1963, while G-APWA saw service with the airline from April to August the same year. *Whisky Alpha* flew on most of the independent's European and Mediterranean holiday routes. In only 33 days from Autair's decision to charter a Herald, ground and aircrew were converted to the type, Ministry of Aviation operating approval was granted, route planning was proved and the first Herald passenger-carrying flight was made.

Autair purposely chose flight crews with no past experience of jet-prop operation and put them through an intensive training programme with outstanding success. Taking ground and flying courses at Handley Page's Radlett Herald school, they converted on to the Herald from DC-3s and Vikings in only three weeks. All six pilots chosen were trained to command level and none required more than six hours flying.

Following route proving trials to destinations such as Lyon, the Herald was introduced into service on regular flights to Greece, Italy, France and Spain. Autair's passengers immediately indicated their preference for the Herald with its smoother, faster flight and high-positioned wing, which gave them fine views of the countryside *en route* to places such as Athens, Naples, Nice, Brindizi, Perpignan, Tarbes, Lyon, Palma and Ibiza.

During the summer season load factors rose to new levels, and often reached 100 per cent. Weekend flying with the chartered Herald averaged 40hr, and at times topped 43hr. During several weekends, 29hr actual flying time was put into a 36hr period, representing first-class serviceability.

In all, nearly 650hr had been flown by the Herald in Autair's hands during weekend flying from Whitsun until the end of September 1963, when the company's summer services were completed. Autair's operations director, Capt M. Rowan, commented: 'During our Herald operations we suffered only one technical delay - and that of a very minor nature at Ibiza. This was quickly rectified by a Handley Page service engineer flown down at only a few minutes' notice in the middle of the night!

'Overall, our flights have gone like clockwork, and we have been most impressed by the aircraft's performance and serviceability.

'With the excellent ground and flying training provided by Handley Page at Radlett, we found no difficulty in converting our DC-3 and Viking crews. In a three-week intensified training programme all our pilots were converted on to the Herald and became greatly impressed by its ease of handling under all conditions.'

At the end of 1963 three Autair captains were based in Amman, instructing aircrew of Alia, the newly-formed Jordanian airline, how to fly the Heralds they had recently acquired from the Royal Jordanian Air Force.

The first ex-BEA machine (G-APWD) arrived at Luton on November 14, 1966, followed two days later by G-APWC and on November 18 by G-APWB. During the winter the airline worked on these aircraft at Luton, repainting and refurnishing them, though they kept the 44-seat passenger configuration. G-APWB was the last of the three to enter passenger service (in November 1967). This aircraft retained its BEA colour scheme, less titling, until at least February 1967.

Autair Series 100 Herald G-APWB (c/n 150) pictured at Luton January 7, 1968. (Philip Birtles)

On March 24, 1967, G-APWC flew north to Glasgow to carry out some ILS training. Four days later it flew its first scheduled service for Autair.

G-APWD was initially used for crew training, staying in BEA colours, less titles, for several months. It was damaged at Luton on take-off for Teesside on September 3, 1967, when it was blown back on to the runway after retracting its undercarriage. By November it was flying again. This aircraft had the distinction of performing Autair's last Heathrow-Leuchars flight (October 30, 1969), and the Heathrow - Leconfield - Teesside flight a day later. On March 27, 1969, it also performed Autair's last scheduled service from Brough prior to transfer of activities to Leconfield.

The Heralds, which supplemented the HS748s when they went on lease to other companies, were based at Luton and linked Luton with Teesside, Heathrow, Brough, RAF Leconfield, Carlisle, Dundee, Amsterdam, Dublin, Belfast, Isle of Man, Jersey and Newquay. They were also used on charters. On April 1, 1969, Teesside became the airline's scheduled services base for maintenance, but not for aircrew. However, in August 1969, after strenuous efforts to obtain subsidies, Autair announced they were to withdraw scheduled services on October 31, 1969, and rely solely on charter and IT work.

The Heralds underwent a nominal change of ownership when Autair was renamed Court Line Aviation Ltd. In 1970 they were placed in open storage at Castle Donington in the care of Fields Aircraft Services while awaiting a buyer. Clarkair International (Services) Ltd acted as exclusive agents for Autair. They offered the three Heralds as a package, together with engines, spare parts and full aircrew and engineering support. Clarkair said the aircraft had been maintained 'to the highest standards' and were available for immediate delivery.

Lineas Aereas La Urraca of Colombia bought them in 1970, and they were overhauled by Fields before delivery. G-APWB had flown 10,465hr and made 15,640 landings by August 1969. It left Luton for Prestwick and Colombia on November 10, 1970, as HK-718. G-APWC had flown 11,154hr and made 15,929 landings by August 1969. It left for Colombia via Prestwick as HK-715 on October 30, 1970, (variously reported as straight from Castle Donington and Luton). G-APWD had flown 10,494hr and made 15,563 landings by August 1969. It was registered HK-721 and flew from Prestwick for delivery to Urraca on October 30, 1970.

The Heralds were ideally suited to Autair's routes. The Teesside-Heathrow run had a 75 per cent load factor in summer and was giving substantial profits, but subsidiary routes had attracted only 10 or 20 passengers per flight.

BRITISH MIDLAND AIRWAYS

Derby Airways took the big step into the jet-prop era when, at the Farnborough air show on September 9, 1964, managing director Mr Ron Paine signed a contract for two Series 200s. A month later Derby Airways was renamed British Midland Airways – the fourth UK operator to order the Herald.

Derby Airways had begun scheduled services from Derby to Jersey after the war. The trusty de Havilland Rapides were joined by Dakotas, and later a fleet of three four-engined Handley Page Marathons was bought, thus forging the first link between the airline and Handley Page.

The airline always believed in 'taking aviation to the people' and that airline service was for everyone, everywhere. Derby Airways expanded quickly and was encouraged by the Marathon's passenger appeal. Larger and faster aircraft were soon needed, so the airline bought several ex-BOAC Canadair Argonaut 78-seaters. These were used on IT flights and charter services as well as on trooping flights.

With their greater comfort, more leg room and faster speed, the Heralds proved particularly suitable for domestic and Channel Islands routes, on which they replaced the Dakotas. Passengers loved the high wing and large oval windows, similar to the Viscount's, which allowed them to watch the passing countryside. From BMA's viewpoint the Herald meant quick turn rounds, economy, easy maintenance and greater flexibility, especially in adaptation for freight carrying.

The latter half of 1964 was a milestone in the airline's history. The combination of a Herald prop-jet fleet and a new and better airport was confidently expected to realise a 50 per cent traffic increase. The first Herald, G-ASKK, entered service on February 1, 1965, after being handed over at Radlett. Just two months later the company's entire establishment was transferred from Burnaston to the new East Midlands Airport at Castle Donington, where it is still based.

However, the entry of the Herald into BMA service was not without problems. It was discovered that G-ASKK had corrosion in the chine 'top hat' section in mid-May 1965, causing pressure differential to be reduced from four to 2.5 p.s.i.

'At the same time another Herald was found to have cuts in skin where ice-guard panel mounting rubber trimmed away, so all Heralds were temporarily depressurised', said BMA's flight safety and security manager, Capt B. G. Cramp.

During modifications to rectify this, BMA's second Herald (G-ATHE) was loaned by Handley Page from August 17 to September 15, 1965. In addition, the much-travelled G-APWA was also loaned at this time, going into service on April 14, 1966, and departing again in September.

The airline's first two Viscounts were obtained from BUA in early 1967, reversing the intended policy of standardising on the Herald. G-ASKK left to go to BU(CI)A on February 15, 1967, in part-exchange.

Later BMA's Herald fleet consisted of three ex-Brazilian machines from Sadia (now Trans Brasil). This resulted from a decision, in 1973, to re-introduce the type. G-ASVO (formerly PP-SDG) left São Paulo on March 14, 1973. Flying from via Brasilia, Carolina, Belem, Cayenne, Barbados, San Juan, Nassau, Miami, Richmond, Bangor, Monkton, Goose Bay, Narsarsuaq, Keflavik and Abbotsinch, it arrived at Castle Donington on March 23, after a total flying time of nearly 48hr. G-ATIG (ex PP-SDI) and G-BAVX (ex PP-SDN) followed shortly after. The three aircraft then spent many weeks on the apron at Castle Donington resting after their long journey from South America until G-BAVX was finally wheeled into BMA's hangar for conversion. It flew again in October.

On November 1, 1975, G-BAVX opened a three-times-a-day Birmingham to Heathrow service in co-operation with British Airways, who operated a daily service on this route. Two Heralds were later based at Aberdeen for much of 1974, operating charter flights on behalf of the many oil companies in the area.

G-ATIG was leased to BIA from April 1, 1975, to October 31, 1975, while Air Anglia wet-leased G-ASVO from October 31, 1975, to March 31, 1976. In 1976 BMA Herald utilisation was 3.8hr per day, the average sector being 250km. BMA doubled its weekly service between EMA and Dublin by substituting Heralds for Viscounts, which were used up to April 1, 1974.

The airline is well-known for its leasing service, individually tailored to each client's particular needs. It has been used by many airlines, and BMA boast a full inventory of aircraft for short- or long-term capacity, including the Viscount and Boeing 707-320.

In 1971 BMA lost over £1,500,000 in a year, but by 1975 this had been transformed into a £500,000 profit. Domestic scheduled services by Heralds, Viscounts and a DC-9 accounted for about 60 per cent of revenue, with passenger load factors running at 55 per cent.

1976 saw the introduction of DC-9s on high load factor routes, the arrival of the first example taking BMA back into the IT field on a modest basis.

Some of the Viscounts will stay in service until well into the 1980s, says managing director Mr Michael Bishop. SAA sold seven Viscounts to BMA in 1972 for £150,000. Unit cost after refurbishing was around £60,000. Bishop says the reason why his airline survives - and grows richer - on expensive short-haul domestic services - is that there is great virtue in being small with modest ambitions. BMA thus avoids confrontations. Slowly but surely it is building for the future on very solid foundations. 1977 marked the 30th anniversary of BMA and its predecessor, Derby Airways, as a domestic scheduled carrier.

BMA had planned to cease all Herald operations from April 1, 1977. G-BAVX was withdrawn from service on September 29, 1976, owing to the very high cost of its next check (Check 4), coupled with undercarriage modifications making it an uneconomical proposition. G-ATIG was operated by Brymon Aviation from January 1, 1977, and G-BAVX and G-ASVO both went to BAF.

BRITISH ISLAND AIRWAYS (AIR UK)

British Island Airways is owned by British Air Transport (Holdings) Ltd, whose shareholders are British and Commonwealth Shipping (90.8 per cent) and Eagle Star Insurance (9.2 per cent). The present company was formed by the amalgamation of three companies; Jersey Airlines, Manx Airlines and Morton Air Services. At the time of the grouping in 1968 the company was a subsidiary of BUA, and was then titled British United Island Airways (BUIA) remaining so until July 1970.

That year, when the owners (British and Commonwealth Group) entered into negotiations for the sale of BUA, BUIA was separated from BUA and given its present name. A new identity for BIA was created, with a new aircraft livery, new badge and new uniforms. The Herald's fins were painted a striking orange, with the BIA logo reversed in white. An orange cheat line was carried along the fuselage from the tail to a point just forward of the mainplane and up to a black BIA logo.

At the end of the first season's operations it was decided to streamline the route network and its aircraft fleet. Some uneconomical routes were dropped, and by 1970 the fleet comprised eight Dart Heralds and three C-47 cargo aircraft. By mid-August 1973 the fleet consisted of 11 Heralds and a solitary C-47. This latter machine (G-AMSV) made its last commercial cargo flight for BIA on May 30, 1974, when it operated service UK842F from Guernsey to Bournemouth. This was an historic occasion in more ways than one, as the Herald had achieved its original purpose of becoming a DC-3 replacement.

Until December 1, 1972, BIA's head office was split between three buildings around the central car park in Redhill, Surrey. The head office has now been centralised in the town's busy High Street, only seven miles from Gatwick and within easy reach of central London. A modern two-storey building, it contains the full management team and the centralised accounts department.

The airline has outstations at Antwerp, Exeter, Guernsey, Isle of Man, Jersey, Southampton and Paris, and its main engineering base is at Blackpool. Reservations control centres have been set up in Blackpool and Redhill, fed by out-of-area telephone lines from major cities in Great Britain and Northern Ireland. This has allowed the airline to provide a more integrated service to travel agents and the public.

BIA operates a network of short-haul scheduled passenger services from the British mainland to the Channel Islands, Isle of Man, Ireland, France and Belgium. Scheduled air cargo services operate between London and Jersey, Guernsey, Dusseldorf and Hanover, and between Bournemouth and Guernsey and London. Air cargo is also carried on the scheduled passenger services. *Ad hoc* charter is a very important facet of the BIA operation. It operates not only individual charters, but also sub-contracted scheduled and passenger and cargo services on behalf of British Caledonian Airways.

BIA also works closely with AERO, the Air Education and Recreation Organisation, providing aerial classrooms for schoolchildren studying geology, history and geography, and at the same time making young people more conscious of air transport.

The airline's alert commercial department is working on numerous developments; one of which is BIA-RAILAIR. In the early 1970s the airline, in conjunction with British Rail, started a publicity campaign to increase public awareness of Southampton airport as the departure point for the Channel Islands. In this scheme the 'RAILAIR' title was coupled with the idea of low cost but speedy transportation between London and the Channel Islands.

In a press release dated April 1973, BIA's then managing director, Bill Elwin, announced that the company had become profitable in 1972, and had for the first time carried more than 500,000 passengers and 11 million kilos of cargo and Royal Mail during the year. In 1973 the number of passengers increased to 550,000. The airline carried 569,340 passengers in 1975, with a healthy overall load factor of 67.2 per cent. Air cargo carried on the special freight routes amounted to over eight million kilos.

In 1976 BIA flew over 540,000 passengers two million miles. Two important new routes were added in 1977 to scheduled passenger services, and cargo and charter operations increased. In cargo configuration BIA's Heralds can carry 4,800 kilos. With a full load of 50 passengers, only 250kg of goods can be uplifted. Without the nightly flights to Jersey and Guernsey with newspapers and mail, breakfast for many islanders would be a very dismal affair.

When B.Cal ceased all its operations to Rotterdam on January 1, 1977, BIA increased its frequency to three flights a day on weekdays in each direction. Rotterdam became the airline's third international destination, and it was anxious to extend its international routes. BIA had started operations to Rotterdam on October 25, 1976, with one return flight each weekday (from Gatwick) in association with B.Cal. It proved a great success with British and Dutch businessmen, who appreciated the extra convenience of flying to and from Gatwick rather than Heathrow.

A Southampton-Le Touquet service was inaugurated on April 1, 1977, spearheading the expansion of overseas flights and intended acquisition of jets. New routes from Gatwick to Frankfurt/Dusseldorf and Geneva/Zurich were being sought, as was a direct Gatwick/Dublin service of 21 flights a week. Aircraft specified in applications to the Civil Aviation Authority were Herald, One-Eleven, DC-9 and Fokker F-28. BIA said they would move into jet equipment if their new route applications, scheduled to be heard by the CAA in June 1977, were approved. The plan was to link Gatwick with six European cities not served by B.Cal – Copenhagen, Hamburg, Frankfurt, Zurich, Geneva and Dublin. BIA thought their request would be in keeping with the Government's promotion of Gatwick as London's second airport. The routes specified paralleled major British Airways trunk routes, but offered more personal service from Gatwick instead of Heathrow.

B.Cal and Dan-Air had submitted similar applications, and British Airways objected to them all. It is probably safe to assume that the national carrier was becoming more and more concerned at the smaller operators offering a service aimed at business travellers.

If the routes were approved, BIA had plans to buy up to five jets, the most likely type being the F-28 Fellowship. The F-28 and DC-9 are relatively quiet and could supplement the Heralds on current routes, and both are more economical than the One-Eleven. Fokker-VFW proposed a common specification and a spares pool to BIA, Air Anglia, Sabena and Netherlands domestic carrier NLM, to help them introduce the new F-28 Mk 4000 to supplement turboprop types. This would cut the cost of aircraft which, in Britain, would be competing against second-hand One-Elevens (100 seats) and DC-9s (80 seats).

The second-hand machines were substantially cheaper to buy than new F-28s, with a One-Eleven going for around $1,200,000 and a DC-9-10 for $2,500,000, compared with around $7m for a new F-28 Mk 4000. But the F-28 has a useful edge in operating costs: it burns less fuel and is lighter, thus cutting landing charges – a major factor on short-haul routes like BIA's.

BIA's interest, however, was conditional on route awards. The six-day hearing, which eventually took place in September 1977, turned down BIA's applications, quickly bringing forth an angry response from airline employees, who accused the CAA of 'bias' and 'siding with the big legions'. The employees said the hearing of the applications was purposely delayed several months so that British Airways could move in. The workers started a campaign and an appeal against the decision was lodged. Said campaign leader Mr Graham King, computer manager at Redhill: 'We submitted our applications in January and March and the hearing was originally set for June.

'Postponed, first 'till July, then again in August, it was eventually heard on September 13, finishing on September 29 after two adjournments, despite the fact that the CAA had promised no adjournments. British Airways put in their applications only 12 days before the final date of the hearing.'

The CAA said that neither BIA or Dan-Air had the 'first division' capability to compete as scheduled service operators on the major connecting routes, and neither had the range or sales outlets and promotional opportunities of BA and B.Cal, enabling them to promote the Gatwick connection round the world.

Some of the BIA routes will never take jets, and the Herald will thus stay in service. The cabin pressure differential has been reduced (to 2.6 p.s.i.), thus 'relifing' the type, and the hull has an indefinite fatigue life.

The airline had told the CAA categorically that they were prepared to invest heavily in new aircraft and in marketing and promotion to ensure the success of new services, if licences were granted. BIA's chairman, the Hon Anthony Cayzer, said in evidence it was important for the long-term well-being of BIA that it should be allowed to develop year-round business routes, thus providing a new stability. Mr Peter Villa, director and general manager of BIA until his appointment as managing director in December 1976, said: 'Once again the CAA has played it safe and sided with the big legions. No airline was prepared to provide Gatwick with the kind of scheduled services it deserves until BIA made its applications – and still isn't. Now, having stirred the State giant into action, we find that we have been squeezed out completely.' The Department of Trade, said Mr Villa in April 1978, was guilty of undue delay in taking action over a decision vital to the future development of the independent airline sector in general and British Island Airways in particular. The Government department, he continued, was dragging its feet on the appeal lodged by the airline over the award of licences to operate European trunk route services from Gatwick.

At the same time Mr Villa accused British Airways of failing to live up to the promises it had made at the time it was confirmed by the Civil Aviation Authority as the British carrier on some of the routes in question. Mr Villa, who was speaking in Amsterdam to guests at a reception to inaugurate the start of BIA scheduled services from Southampton on May 2, said: 'It is ironic that, of all the routes for which we applied last year, this is the only one that the Civil Aviation Authority has granted us leave to operate so far. Those of you with long memories will recall that we formally applied between January and March 1977 to the Civil Aviation Authority to operate from Gatwick to Frankfurt, Hamburg, Copenhagen, Zurich, Geneva and Dublin. It took us until September – yes, as long as eight months – to get a hearing from the CAA, and in the meantime, of course, other airlines, notably British Airways and British Caledonian, jumped on the bandwagon.

'Until we showed our hand neither of these airlines had made any attempt to apply for these services which Gatwick needed and, if its full potential as the second London Airport is to be realised, undoubtedly deserves. When the CAA finally announced its decision on October 26, British Airways and British Caledonian emerged – with hindsight one could almost say predictably – as the airlines selected to operate to the destinations for which we had applied.

'To say we were bitterly disappointed is an understatement. Nevertheless, so confident were we that justice had not been done and in the strength of our case, that on November 11 we filed an appeal with the Secretary of State for Trade asking him to overturn the CAA decision. That was more than five long months ago. Since then, despite our inquiries to the Department of Trade, we have been confronted by a wall of silence. And in the interim, of course, if it had lived up to its promises of dedicated commitment to Gatwick that it made to the CAA, British Airways should have launched services to some of the points for which we had applied.

'What has happened? All the travelling public has got is a token service to Zurich. There is still no word from the national carrier as to when, precisely, it plans to operate its promised services to Frankfurt, Dublin and Dusseldorf despite assurances given to the CAA at the time of the hearing that they would be started in April. What would have happened if BIA had been granted the routes within a reasonable time scale? There would now have been at least two return services a day from Gatwick to Zurich, Frankfurt and Dublin. To Geneva and Hamburg there would have been at least one return service a day. And we would still have been here today celebrating next week's launch of the Southampton/Amsterdam route.

'We in BIA interpret the Department of Trade's lack of action on our appeal as symptomatic of the Government's attitude towards the independent sector as a whole . . . We see it as being wholly out of step with the Department's latest airport policy White Paper, which advocates the use of quieter aircraft. BIA proposed the use of the Fokker F-28 Fellowship, a quiet aircraft which meets the most stringent noise requirements.

'It is a sad fact that in Government civil aviation policy the needs of the national carrier and British Caledonian, as the second force, are deemed paramount and the hopes and aspirations of airlines such as ourselves are treated with apparent disdain.

'Maybe we should have predicted the result of the hearing. You can draw your own conclusions. But one thing that an experience such as this does for BIA is that when we are successful in winning a new route, everything within our power is done to ensure its success – of that you can be sure.'

BIA bought British and lost its fight all within a week. For it purchased three One-Elevens from Gulf Air and heard its appeal against the decision had been dismissed.

Said Mr Villa: 'We explored other areas of development, as so far we have been denied the opportunity to enlarge our scheduled service network from Gatwick. Investigations showed there was a lack of short-to-medium haul aircraft for the British inclusive tour market.'

To add insult to injury, the first Villa heard of the appeal was reading about it in the national press. A written reply arrived later – by second class post.

While the new One-Elevens travel twice as fast and far as the Heralds, they will not be used for cargo operations, as they are not quick-change aircraft. Mr Villa says 'When it comes to carrying cargo our Heralds suit us down to the ground. They can be converted in minutes'.

In 1977 BIA carried 563,000 passengers for an average load factor of 61.2 per cent, flew more than 73½ million passenger miles and had a turnover of £11 million. Cargo represented a quarter of the turnover. The year still gave BIA – and the public – a lot to smile about. The airline ran a poster campaign in London and the south-east in a light-hearted but informative style. Examples that brought a grin to rail commuters included 'BIA Gatwick-Rotterdam pick-me-up taken three times a day'; 'Clever clogs fly BIA to Rotterdam 17 times a week from Gatwick'; and 'Guernsey weightlifter relaxes after picking up BIA plane at Southampton'.

1977 also saw a face-lift for the Heralds. The airline was due for a new paint scheme, and various Heralds were painted up in different colours until a new livery was decided upon. The airline adopted a more conscious public identity by dropping 'BIA' in favour of British Island Airways on the fuselage – the first time the carrier's name had appeared in full.

In September 1976 G-APWF was painted in a trial livery, keeping the orange cheatline but featuring an all-white tail fin on which appeared the logo 'British Island' in black. *Whisky Foxtrot* also appeared with an orange and brown band sweeping up the fin, broken by the words 'British Island'. The registration was painted on the fin fillet.

At the BIA maintenance base at Blackpool, Squires Gate, in March 1977, sister ship G-APWE was painted in the new livery, rather similar to the old BUIA scheme. It comprised an orange cheat line with brown trim lines either side of the main band, on a white fuselage and fin. The cheat and trim lines swept along the fuselage and up the fin, BIA lettering in brown appearing diagonally on the fin parallel to the top brown trim line. Below the lower brown trim line 'British Island Airways' appeared in black.

The fleet was gradually painted up in the new colours as it went in for major maintenance. By January 1978, at least 'WE, 'WF and G-BBXI had been re-painted.

A highly significant milestone for BIA was when Air Anglia agreed to be taken over by BIA's owners, the British and Commonwealth Shipping Group. The move, announced late in 1978, meant that both airlines would still be run separately, but there was scope for co-operation in planning future jet fleets.

From January 1, 1979, BIA also took over the scheduled services operated by BAF from Southend (q.v.). These moves created one of the biggest regional airline groups in Europe.

Months of speculation ended late in 1979 with the news that BIA and Air Anglia were to merge. The decision came much sooner than most people thought it would. But what would British & Commonwealth call their new creation? British United Airways? Possibly British Isles Airways (to keep the initials of BIA?).

No 'informed source' came up with the right answer – Air UK. When Air Anglia was added to B & C's airline inventory in October 1978 for a reported £2,750,000, the plan was to keep BIA and Air Anglia as separate companies. By early 1980 they had been merged completely.

Air UK also comprises BIA/Air West and Air Wales, two third-level carriers, and is now the third largest UK scheduled carrier (after British Airways and British Caledonian).

The bringing together of these operators under one umbrella means that half of the 42 aircraft in the fleet are Heralds. The remainder include F-27s, F-28s,

One-Elevens and Bandeirantes. BIA managing director Peter Villa became the new Air UK managing director, while chairman is the Hon Anthony Cayzer. Rumours late in 1979 that the F-27s and F-28s were to be disposed of and the fleet rationalised around the Heralds and One-Elevens were dismissed by Villa.

Air UK was conceived at the time when British Airways decided to shed its loss-making regional services and slim down its profile, to appear perhaps a more profitable investment after announcing it was going public.

The 26 'second-level' routes to provincial cities and towns were mostly flown by fuel-guzzling Viscounts, now an economic embarrassment for BA, which estimates it loses around £4 million every year flying 800,000 people on the routes. Air UK applied for nine of the BA routes axed in April 1980.

The new independent will spread its wings to all corners of the UK as well as Continental destinations. It expects to carry more than 1,500,000 passengers and to achieve a turnover of £50 million within its first year. Air UK will concentrate on developing routes that bigger airlines might not find profitable.

It will serve 23 airports in the UK and nine on the Continent, including Amsterdam, Paris and Frankfurt. Major centres of operation will be at Gatwick, Southend, Norwich, the Channel Islands, Southampton, Blackpool, Isle of Man, Edinburgh and Aberdeen.

Said Villa: 'By bringing together the operations of the three airlines we are creating a new and powerful force in British air transport. However, our policy in doing so is not borne on the premise that "big is beautiful". This new company, with its streamlined and integrated services, will be better placed to trade successfully in these difficult days of increasing costs and fare competition. We believe the potential for the airline is enormous. Already many of the routes operated by Air Anglia and BIA have proved the ever-increasing regional demands for air services, both domestic and international.'

November 1979 was when Air UK revealed how it aimed to present itself to the world. Appropriately enough, the first aircraft to sport the eye-catching new livery was a Herald. The dominant colour is blue, complemented by a striking white and red cheat line. The Air UK logo is surmounted by a futuristic winged symbol. First to fly the patriotic colours, G-BAZJ, made its first flight as such on November 19 from Blackpool. G-BEBB was being painted up at Southend about the same time.

Said Villa: 'Having adopted the name Air UK we thought it right and proper to wave a truly nationalistic flag by painting our aircraft red, white and blue. We will be carrying the Union flag colours to wherever we fly.'

For some time speculation has been rife as to whether the airline will eventually dispose of its Heralds and standardise on a fleet of F-27s. It seems that the Heralds will go - eventually - and the F-27s will stay. But as to exactly when depends on the number of landings an aircraft has accumulated, not the hours.

BRITISH AIR FERRIES

British Air Ferries was formed in January 1963 by the merger of Channel Air Bridge (founded 1959) and Silver City Airways (founded 1948). Both operated cross-Channel vehicle and passenger ferry services. The merged company was known as British United Air Ferries Ltd until 1967, when the present title was adopted. BAF was owned by Air Holdings Ltd until October 1971, when the company was acquired by Mr T. D. Keegan.

Shareholding is held by T. D. Keegan (90 per cent) and C.A.B. St George (10 per cent). Scheduled passenger-cargo services are operated from Southend airport to Le Touquet, Ostend, Rotterdam and Basle and Dusseldorf. An associate company, BAF Engineering Ltd, undertakes extensive maintenance, overhaul and repair services.

In the early 'sixties air ferry traffic across the Channel was in a healthy state. In 1962 it reached a peak of 137,000 cars, but the figure had dropped to 109,000 by 1964, and to 101,000 two years later. One of the main reasons was that cross-Channel surface transport had been revitalised and improved, creating fierce competition. So a combination of passengers, cars and freight was seen to be the correct formula for future expansion.

European freight services were much in demand for an aircraft like the Carvair, which could carry anything from a ship's propeller to several tons of tomatoes from the Channel Islands. Dutch bulbs, jet engines and even, on one occasion, a live three-ton killer whale, have been transported, as well as pop groups and their equipment.

The Carvair, an original re-design of the DC-4, involved extending the nose by 8ft 6in and fitting nose-loading cargo doors with the cockpit above. First flight of this 'new' aircraft, called the ATL.98 Carvair, was on June 21, 1961. The aeroplane replaced the ageing Bristol Freighters which had been operated since 1948, but it was now the faithful Carvair's turn to bow out. Passenger services were withdrawn late in 1976, leaving just three Carvairs in service for freighting.

A foretaste of things to come was seen in 1970, when two HS748s (a traditional rival to the Herald) were put into operation. It was the second aircraft BAF had operated that could not carry cars (being pipped at the post by a leased Viscount).

The airline's commitment to the Herald became apparent in January 1975, when the purchase of their first three (from Eastern Provincial Airways of Canada) was finalised. G-BCWE *Jeremy Keegan*, ex CF-EPI arrived at Southend on January 28, and started crew training with the help of BIA on February 4. On February 20 a service was flown from Southend to Rotterdam. The second Herald, G-BCZG *Rupert Keegan*, ex CF-NAC was delivered in March.

The last, G-BDFE *Rory Keegan*, ex CF-EPC, was extensively overhauled like the others and refurbished for conversion to a 21-seat VIP fit (q.v.). The Heralds, originally to have been delivered in January, February and March 1975, in time for the summer schedules, were named after the three sons of BAF's chairman, Mr T. D. (Mike) Keegan. The introduction of the Heralds on the airline's scheduled services meant that more of the ageing Carvairs could be

G-BCWE *Jeremy Keegan* (c/n 166) in the original BAF Herald paint scheme. (BAF)

turned into freighters.

In January 1976 BAF was negotiating for a fourth Herald (from Arkia). Other reports suggested that two more Heralds were on option from an undisclosed company for delivery in 1977.

During the visit of the Brazilian President to Britain in 1976, the purchase of three Heralds plus supporting spares was concluded between BAF and TransBrasil. These were the last three Heralds to be operated by the Brazilian airline (formerly Sadia). G-BDZV (ex PP-SDL) was delivered on June 30, rolled out July 12, and received its C of A on July 16. It entered service the same day. G-BEBB (ex PP-SDH) arrived on July 15, while the former demonstrator G-APWA (ex PP-SDM) arrived on August 11. G-BEBB entered service on September 26.

During the same year the whole airline was given a 'face-lift' with a striking new 'wasp' livery, with two mustard-coloured hoops separated by a blue band (similar to that of the maritime F-27). First to be so painted was G-BDZV. New staff uniforms were also introduced.

Again in 1976, BAF applied for licences from Birmingham and Manchester to Rotterdam and Antwerp, from Southend to Dusseldorf and Lille, and for a daily service to Basle via Luxembourg.

The Heralds were operated as 26-seaters, with capacity for two-and-a-half tons of cargo in the forward section. A quick-shift bulkhead allowed the ratio of passengers to cargo to be varied during a 30min turnround. The Brazilian Heralds were similarly modified.

1976 certainly stood out as an active year for BAF, for the airline also turned its Herald-orientated eyes to the Royal Malaysian Air Force military Heralds, which had been replaced by Hercules transports. Negotiations proceeded to buy all eight, and possibly convert them to pax/cargo use, with two as freighters for use in Scotland.

The globe-trotting G-APWA made a welcome return to the shores of its birth in 1976. Engineering officer Lenny Kent well remembers the time he went out to Brazil to bring back the first production Herald.

'Technically it was a disaster. The air conditioning would not work, pressurisation was defective, and there were hydraulic leaks. It took 20,000 man-hours before *Whisky Alpha* got its C of A just before Easter 1977,' he recalls.

'The radio side was also a complete disaster. We thought we would never iron out the problems.' But BAF did. The airline hopes to keep the Herald flying for several years to come.

Said Lenny Kent: 'The trip back home took 11 days, and the Herald flew very well. We brought back two tons of spares. The route was via São Paulo, Brasilia, Belem, Cayenne (French Guiana), Barbados, Puerto Rico, New Barbados, New York, Sept Iles (Quebec), Fort Chimo (an Eskimo village in N. Canada) then on to Baffin Island (Frobisher Bay), Sonderstrom, Reykjavik, Leeds and Southend.' Captain on the ferry flight was John Baard, and first officer Scott Crawford.

Rumour has it that *Whisky Alpha* wore its khaki and almost day-glo colour scheme in case it crashed in the jungle territory over which it often flew in Brazil. It would certainly have been easier to see.

A metal plaque at the rear of the cabin gives details of the Herald's association with Prince Philip (spelt with two 'ls'!) The former Brazilian Heralds reveal their origins to the observant passenger by their 'No Smoking –

Two Heralds at Le Touquet. Note the stationary train in front of G-BDFE (c/n 167).

Nao Fume' and 'Fasten Seat Belts - Apertar Os Cintos' signs.

G-APWA flew its first revenue flight for BAF on April 11 1977 - as a 44-seater. At the Blackbushe Air Festival on July 30/31 several joyriders paid their fivers for a 15min flight over the Hampshire countryside in 'WA.

Lenny Kent also flew back with the former EPA Herald CF-EPC (G-BDFE) after it had made a wheels-up landing on Prince Edward Island on February 8, 1975.

'The accident had ripped the belly, and it was thought a write-off. But the plane was bought off the insurance company for one Canadian dollar. We arrived back at Southend from Moncton, Gander and Reykjavik. The Reykjavik-Southend sector was probably one of the longest Herald flights ever - it took 4hr 50min, and when we got back to England there was no fuel left in the tanks.' The crew on this flight comprised Capt Bernie Warrmen, first officer Samuel Areskie, in addition to Lenny Kent.

In the late 1970s Southend became a hive of Heralds, emphasised by the 'Buzz off with BAF' slogan of the airline. BAF bought the two remaining BMA Heralds, increasing their Herald fleet from three to eight in a year. G-ASVO and G-BAVX both arrived in January 1977. The following year 15 Heralds were in service, operating scheduled services, European charters and wet lease operations in the Middle East.

From January 1977 the car ferry service ceased and the last Carvairs were put up for sale. The stalwart Carvairs were withdrawn on January 1, bringing to an end car ferry services begun in 1948. They represented only five per cent of sales in 1976.

Plain Jane was stripped of all paintwork and interior fittings (apart from five seats) and converted into a pure freighter. Up to five double horse boxes could be accommodated in the cargo hold.

BAF re-introduced a Southend-Calais service twice daily from December 1, 1976, using Heralds. This route was dropped in 1971 because of fall-off in demand and rising operating costs, but was revived due to the erosion of the fare differential between air and sea travel. The upturn in general business traffic between the south-east and the Calais-Dunkirk catchment areas confirmed the airline's belief in the route's viability. In the event the route was not well used, and a leased Dove (G-BBYA ex Air Lynx) was substituted before the service was finally dropped because it was not paying.

BAF had the distinction of becoming the world's largest-ever Herald operator when the eight former Royal Malaysian Air Force Series 400 Heralds were acquired. The deal was rather complicated, as Hants and Sussex Aviation successfully bid for the planes in 1977, then Bembridge Air Hire (a Keegan Group company) bought the Heralds in turn from Hants and Sussex. It was reported that BAF originally bid £500,000 for the package. Said Jeremy Keegan in March 1977: 'We have bid for the RMAF Heralds, seven of which are in flying condition and one of which is quite badly damaged.' He denied suggestions his company had negotiated for the Arkia Heralds then up for disposal. G-BEYI (FM-1025) had been in an accident at Butterworth, and after considerable deliberation the hulk was cannabilised, as it was not worthy of recovery.

BAF intended using four of the Heralds on their own scheduled and charter services, and to offer the others for wet or dry lease. There was no apparent urgency to bring home the aircraft, which had been standing in the hot jungle at Kuala Lumpur for many months, except for the first two, as charter work was booming.

The first, G-BEYF (FM-1022) came back in August 1977, followed a month later by G-BEYG (FM-1023). They were ferried back at the rate of approximately one a month, in painted-out RMAF livery with the new registrations on the fuselage. The engines were taken out at Southend, and replaced by new units from BAF's stock.

The Heralds were registered to some weird and unusual-sounding company names, concealing the identity of the real operator. Four were listed to Bembridge Air Hire Ltd, two to Killyspae Ltd, another to African Safari Travel Ltd and the eighth to Staymond Investments Ltd - all the owners' names were merely pseudonyms for Mike Keegan's companies, and the Heralds were registered to members of the Keegan group.

Yankee Foxtrot made engine runs in full BAF livery on September 29. In just seven weeks all major modifications had been completed and 'YF became the first to be civilianised. BAF Engineering Ltd undertook the refurbishing and maintenance, including the fitting of a completely new interior with modifications to the bulkheads and galley. A C of A was granted in early October.

'YF was put on Continental scheduled services on October 4. Less than two weeks later she was off to Gulf Air in the Middle East on lease for several months. Said Capt John Woodhouse, BAF's operations director: 'In 1978 we leased 'YF to BIA for approximately eight months. The Herald had already been "BAFised", and this presented them with considerable problems of incorporating it into their operation in view of the fact it is a 401 series, compared to the 200 series which they are currently operating.'

'YD arrived at Southend on October 18, 1977, fitted with long-range tanks, followed by 'YE on November 14. The author was lucky enough to fly in *Yankee Echo* on the long ferry flight from Kuala Lumpur.

Next home was 'YJ, which arrived just before Christmas, with 'YH following on January 18, 1978. Last to arrive at Southend was 'YK, on March 5. Shortly afterwards this Herald was sold to BIA and was accepted ex Malaysia.

Transmeridian Air Cargo (TAC), formerly part of the T. D. Keegan airline group, was sold to the Cunard Shipping Company for £3.37 million during 1977. Keegan's interest remains with BAF, which stays under his ownership. Mike Keegan did, however, threaten that he would sell up rather than be obliged to recognise the British Air Line Pilots' Association.

After months of speculation, BIA announced late in 1978 that from January 1, 1979, it would take over scheduled services operated by BAF out of Southend, together with half of BAF's Heralds on long-term lease. BIA also absorbed about 140 BAF staff made redundant by the dropping of scheduled international services – Southend to Basle, Dusseldorf, Ostend, Rotterdam and Le Touquet, and from Manchester to Rotterdam.

BAF gave up scheduled services because its limited route network became harder to operate at a profit in view of ever-growing costs. A spokesman for the airline said that by combining with another operator of a similar aircraft type, the unified operation made sound commercial sense. To cope with the expansion, BIA leased seven Heralds from BAF, thus bringing its Herald fleet up to 20.

BIA cargo operations were given a major boost by the route transfer. Said a BIA spokesman: 'Southend is very similar to Southampton, which we already operate from. It is a small airport with good relations and so there is less chance of delays.' For BIA, the integration added another six international routes to an extensive network which covers 19 destinations, and on which in 1977 carried 562,000 passengers. It added another 134 services to the 290 a week already operated by BIA.

BAF Engineering overhauled and converted Herald Series 400 G-BEYG to an all-cargo configuration during 1978 – the first Herald ever to be so modified. It now has a payload of 5,918 kilos, with 38.5 cubic metres of usable volume. Lashing points are built into the 16.4 metre floor, and the pressurisation system has been retained so that the Herald can still fly at high altitudes.

The 'changed role' Herald proved a great success in its first two weeks of flying. Heralds had only 2,500 kilos capacity when flying in the mixed passenger/cargo role.

Owing to the time taken removing and refitting passenger seats in Heralds used on nightly newspaper runs, plus the wear, tear and damages to the seats themselves, G-BEYG (and possibly 'YH) was re-configured. *Yankee Golf* was test-flown on September 10, 1978, and entered service on the 14th. All cabin windows have been blacked out (except for one each side), and the word CARGO is carried in yellow after the main fuselage titles in blue. It is thought this Herald took over from 'YJ as Herald crew trainer, allowing that aircraft to be overhauled next. In an attempt to keep the engineering department occupied after all the military Heralds had passed through, BAF advertised for Viscounts, HS748s and F-27s, preferably needing major overhauls, for eventual re-sale.

Nightly newspaper flights from Southend to Newcastle, carrying *The Sun*, began on September 22, 1978, (first used was G-BEBB). The charter is operated Tuesdays to Saturdays inclusive, and newspaper flights are also flown to Dusseldorf, Hanover, Aldergrove and Paris.

Leases and charters are becoming so prolific that it is difficult to record them all. However, G-BAVX was operated for SATA in the Azores from mid-October 1978 due to that airline's pilots' strike. G-BDFE left Southend for EAS on December 2, 1978, returning on the 12th.

G-BEYJ was withdrawn from crew training and stored engineless at the same time 'YH entered the hangar.

The six Heralds transferred to BIA were G-ASVO, 'BCWE, 'BCZG, 'BDZV, 'BEBB and 'BEYF. G-BCWE was rolled out on December 8, 1978, entering service four days later on a newspaper run. This aircraft and 'YF were in full BIA colours, with the others carrying BIA on the tail instead of BAF and British Island Airways in place of British Air Ferries on the fuselage. G-BEYD was the seventh Herald to go to BIA (on April 1, 1979).

G-APWE arrived at Southend for service on December 4, 1978, becoming the first of the BIA fleet to be worked on at Southend.

Jeremy Keegan is convinced that his airline did right in letting BIA take over the short-haul routes. 1979 saw the chartering and leasing of Heralds charge ahead in top gear. A leasing operator was never without an aircraft, as Heralds were rotated and replaced as they were serviced.

Leasing costs at least £15,000 per month, much less than rival F-27s or 748s. Heralds were purchased to take over from the Carvairs, and in early 1979 BAF's last three examples of this unique aircraft were up for sale or lease 'within the next six months'. Cargo started to account for up to half of BAF's business, so the decision to concentrate purely on charter and leasing made sound economic sense.

Scheduled services demand far more staff, and overheads are high. The new low fares, and probable de-regulation following the pattern set in the US with many small companies starting up, means a boom in the leasing market. So what of the future? The chances are BAF will pick a winner again when the time comes to re-equip.

During 1979, the Heralds were leased out to various operators. 'Yours to command' Heralds by the hour, day, week or even year flew services for Nile Valley Aviation, TAT, SATA (in the Azores) and Brymon, among others.

The 14 Heralds were offered in a variety of configurations: all freight (up to 5.95 tonnes), all passenger (50 seats) or passenger/freight in multiples of four reducing down to a minimum of 16 seats. They could be leased dry or wet with or without full maintenance support. BAF also train or convert a company's own flight and cabin crews.

By December 1979 BAF was offering a 'matched fleet' of four Heralds available for sale, wet or dry lease (G-BEYE, 'YG, 'YH and 'YJ). G-BEYD was returned to BAF in January 1980. Air UK (q.v.) bought four F-27 Friendships from Touraine Air Transport, replacing four Heralds leased from BAF, in 1980. They were phased into use between March and June.

AIR ANGLIA

Air Anglia Ltd was formed on August 1, 1970, by the merger of three charter and air taxi operators: Norfolk Airways, Anglian Air Charter and Rig Air. The company had the backing of the Norwich Union Insurance Group. Scheduled passenger services, inaugurated in 1971, were operated along with charter and IT flights, mainly for Anglia Holidays, a subsidiary company.

Apart from a mixed bag of Piper aircraft, the airline also operated a fleet of Fokker Friendships. Herald G-ASVO was wet-leased from BMA in 1975, starting scheduled services on March 2 and operating in Air Anglia livery. Daily routes operated by the Herald between March and early November were between Norwich, Leeds, Edinburgh, Aberdeen, Bergen, Aberdeen, Edinburgh, Leeds and Norwich, and from November 3, 1975, the aircraft operated Norwich, Amsterdam, Norwich, Teesside, Newcastle, Aberdeen, Newcastle, Teesside, Norwich, Amsterdam, Norwich.

'From early June 1975 the plane was operated by our own aircrews on dry lease from BMA and was included on our Air Operators Certificate during early July', said deputy operations services manager Mr P. G. Walton.

'The main reason for operating the Herald was that, at the beginning of 1975, a time when our scheduled routes were expanding, it was not possible to buy another F-27 Series 200 due to world-wide demand for the type.

'This meant a temporary lease of a similar type, which resulted in the Handley Page Herald joining our fleet of five F-27 aircraft.'

It was intended to replace the Herald with an F-27 as soon as a suitable aircraft could be located. Air Anglia only leased the one Herald from BMA, although G-BAVX in BMA livery was occasionally used on their routes during March, April and May 1975, when G-ASVO was off-line for maintenance and checks. A Humberside to Jersey scheduled service was opened by G-ASVO on April 19, 1975.

The F-27s Air Anglia sought were harder to find than anticipated, so the Herald lease was extended several times. It finally went back to BMA on March 31, 1976. Air Anglia would have liked G-ASVO to stay another month, but the aircraft was needed by BMA for its own scheduled services.

Air Anglia leased G-ASVO (c/n 185) for a short period. Painted up in full Air Anglia colours, 'VO is seen at Newcastle February 13, 1976. (Ian MacFarlane)

British Air Ferries then came to the rescue by leasing Herald G-BCWE to the airline for six weeks from April 1, 1976. The Herald was favoured by Air Anglia and, in the best tradition of the type, gave few problems. There were a few minor upsets when the 50 seats in the Herald were sold before it was realised that its place was to be taken by a Friendship, which seats only 44.

BRYMON AIRWAYS

Brymon Airways, the West Country-based third level airline, joined the ranks of Herald operators in 1977, albeit in a small way. When British Midland Airways sold off its three Heralds, Brymon's managing director and principal shareholder, Capt Bill Bryce, saw his opportunity to take over a ready-made service to London from Newquay. The airline bought G-ATIG together with operating crew and handling rights to link Newquay with Heathrow, 75min flying time away, five days a week. Newquay was the only airport in the area which could take the twin-turboprop.

Brymon was quickly granted the licence to fly the route previously serviced by BMA. Industrial action caused by redundancies at BMA meant that the East Midlands-based airline operated the service for another week. Finally, on January 10, 1977, G-ATIG, resplendent in its new, eye-catching livery of white and grey with yellow and blue cheat line, operated its first service with its new owner.

Brymon Aviation was formed in March 1969 by Capt Bryce and racing driver Chris Amon, 'Brymon' being derived from an amalgamation of the owners' names. An associate company, Brymon Airports Ltd, controls and

Brymon Airways bought a Herald from BMA. G-ATIG (c/n 177) is still in service with this West Country airline. (APN)

administers Plymouth City Airport and the Newquay Airport Civil Terminal.

Brymon began operating in the summer of 1972 on a seasonal basis between the Scilly Isles, Newquay (optional stop), Plymouth and Jersey. Services are now flown all year round with Islanders and Twin Otters over routes such as Plymouth to Jersey and Guernsey, Plymouth to Morlaix and Newquay to Plymouth.

In 1976 30,000 passengers were carried. The introduction of the Herald doubled these figures for 1977. The airline flew 22,500 revenue passengers during the first six months of 1977 – more than doubling its 1976 performance. The Twin Otters and Islanders have a utilisation rate of more than 1,000hr a year, much higher than the Herald, which is only used on the Newquay-London route. When G-ATIG has been on overhaul by Fields at East Midlands Airport, the service has been flown by BAF Heralds.

In August 1977 Brymon advertised the 50-seat Herald for immediate dry lease.

Not only was Brymon the first British operator of the Twin Otter – it also placed the first British order for the Twin Otter's big brother, the 50-seat Dash 7. The order, worth over £2 million, is the biggest investment ever made by this growing airline.

In December 1978 Brymon announced that it had been awarded the Newquay to Aberdeen service. Scheduled to have been inaugurated by April 1, 1979, the weekday service sees greater utilisation of the Herald between the morning and evening Newquay-Heathrow service.

The airline started their Newquay-Aberdeen service April 2, 1979, initially operating twice weekly on Mondays and Fridays. An extra flight on Wednesdays was under serious consideration, as was the replacement of the Herald, which took some 2½hr to cover the UK's longest domestic route. The Wednesday sevice was introduced on June 6.

Most likely candidate is the Boeing 737, which was being suggested by several of Brymon's staff at a press conference to mark the inaugural flight.

EXPRESS AIR FREIGHT/SERVICES

Heralds ushered in a new era of Channel Islands flower power when Express Air Freight of Guernsey bought two of the Arkia Heralds in 1977. The aircraft were operated by Intra Airways on behalf of EAF, and flew the Jersey flower run to East Midlands and Bournemouth. The ex-Israeli Heralds were repatriated to the UK and delivered to Castle Donington in mid-1977, where they underwent a major overhaul before going into service.

Each had a 4½ tonne capacity, and they replaced two DC-3s (G-AKNB and G-AMPZ). Peterport Aviation Ltd, Guernsey-based contractors to overseas governments and airline operators, advertised the two 50-seat Heralds for sale in *Flight International* during April 1977, with immediate availability. In part, the advertisement read: 'Pressurised with DIFF pressure recorders fitted and fully modified to latest standards. Offered with half-life engines and possibility of a package with spares included'.

During September 1977 there was a certain air of mystery as to the eventual destination of the two Heralds. Reports from various sources seemed to indicate Intra had denied they were buying the aircraft, while others said Intra was to get two BMA Viscounts, so making the Heralds superfluous. As far back as 1974 there was a suggestion that Intra might replace its DC-3s with . . . Heralds!

In the event, the two were registered to Field Aviation Ltd and overhauled and prepared for service at East Midlands Airport by Fields. EAF is a subsidiary of Field Aircraft Services. G-BEZB (4X-AHS) was registered on August 2, 1977, and its Israeli markings removed. G-ATDS (4X-AHT) arrived via Lyon on July 28, and was painted as G-ATDS on September 7.

Evidently Arkia, because of financial difficulties and an over-capacity problem with the introduction of the One-Eleven, had cut a number of services and sold the Heralds.

The new operator took delivery of G-ATDS and G-BEZB at Hurn during December 1977/January 1978, the first Channel Islands cargo service being operated on January 15.

On December 10, 1977, G-BEZB arrived at Southend for crew training conducted by BAF. This was completed by January 13 and 'ZB was delivered to Hurn the following day by BAF crew.

The Argosies of Air-Bridge Carriers which used to ply this route were withdrawn because of structural problems, and the Heralds were substituted on these scheduled services. So ABC began operating a daily service to Jersey and Guernsey in association with EAF from Castle Donington. (ABC is also a

Express Air Freight acquired four Heralds from the Israeli internal airline, Arkia. Here G-BEZB (c/n 174) rests at East Midlands Airport in October 1977. (MAP)

subsidiary of Field Aircraft Services).

Thanks to the Heralds, cargo from Britain can be delivered in the Channel Islands within a day, resulting in a freight boom. This operation involves Express Air, which formed Express Air Freight, Island Express Transport and Roadline. Goods from the mainland are trunked to Roadline at Portsmouth and Bournemouth. From here packages are forwarded on by air or sea, the customs are cleared and then they are delivered by Island Express in Jersey or Express Air in Guernsey.

EAF managing director Mr Peter Glenister explained that Roadline moved southbound cargo from the mainland via the airline, which delivered the goods on the islands with its own haulage fleet. The link-up certainly made business sense. Before this partnership Heralds flew in flowers and produce to Bournemouth, but returned empty.

EAF also acquired the other pair of Arkia Heralds. G-BFRJ (4X-AHO) was delivered via Lyon to Castle Donington on March 30, 1978, and G-BFRK (4X-AHN) followed on April 6. The Heralds were offered with half-life engines and props together with complete support spares package, ground equipment and tools and advertised as 'suitable for operators wishing to establish new operation'.

Shortly afterwards, Express Air Services (the title used when passengers are carried) advertised for captains and first officers because of fleet expansion. 4X-AHO and 'HN were held on option by ABC, which told *Flight International* in August 1977 that it knew of no plans by Intra to acquire the aircraft.

The first passenger sub-charter was on March 17, 1978, when G-ATDS operated the Bournemouth-Jersey-Bournemouth run five times for Dan-Air. Later that year, EAS Heralds kept the north-east posted when the Post Office had to charter aircraft to carry mail. Nightly flights from Gatwick to Newcastle and Gatwick to RAF Leeming in North Yorkshire began on September 11. This was because two railway tunnels on the main east coast line from the capital to Newcastle were closed due to engineering works. November 3 saw the last Newcastle-Gatwick-Newcastle air mail flight using G-BFRJ. EAS resumed NCL-LGW-NCL Royal Mail flights on November 20, after being operated to Stansted.

It was reported that the Express Air Freight (CI) group of companies and Intra Airways merged in early 1979. Field Aviation, a wholly-owned subsidiary of the Hunting Group of public companies, had a stake in EAF, while ABC worked closely with EAF so the merger meant a many-aspected organisation.

The EAF (CI) group included Express Air Services, Carpenter's Air Services (1975) and Carpenter's Transport. The new company brought together a fleet of Viscounts and DC-3s, the four Heralds, and Viscount, Argosy and Vanguard aircraft operated by Field.

In February 1979 Intra advertised for Gatwick-based Viscount captains and first officers, Herald captains and first officers to be based at Bournemouth or Jersey, DC-3 captains and first officers to be based at Jersey, and cabin staff for Viscounts and Heralds to be based in Jersey, Bournemouth or Gatwick.

Joint managing directors of Intra and its subsidiary are now Peter Glenister, managing director EAF and its subsidiaries, and John Capstick, a member of the main Hunting board and a director of Field Aviation. Intra's previous managing director, Bernard Haddican, became director responsible for operations and engineering. Art Carpenter, founder of Carpenter's Air Services, carried on as Express director responsible for all Guernsey operations.

Intra Airways changed its name to Jersey European Airways on November 1 1979 – 'heralding' plans to expand services from Jersey and Southampton.

The remaining pair of DC-3s were due to be replaced early in 1980 by 20-seat Bandeirantes. The three-strong Viscount fleet was bolstered by the addition of the four Heralds previously operated by EAS.

The renaming came about after a review of Intra's operations since it merged in January 1979 with the Express Air Freight (CI) group and became associated with Field Aviation.

Jersey European would like to operate new routes, especially short-range services to Europe. The airline applied for the Southampton-Jersey route dropped by British Airways, as well as Southampton to Glasgow, Liverpool and Dinard using Viscounts/Heralds. It applied to the CAA for most of the routes BA proposed to relinquish. Intra believed that it was not in Jersey's interests to have no control over their future by allowing UK operators to take over a monopoly of the major routes serving the Channel Islands.

The Channel Islands Tour Operators Group wanted the Guernsey and Jersey Governments to work together and run their own airline to keep up the London link. CITOG argued that the two islands could lease aircraft with

Shannon, June 1978 – Herald G-BFRJ (c/n 195) in Air Ecosse livery. (MAP/D.O' Mahony)

crews and fly services into Heathrow at times (and prices) to suit islanders.

Jersey European's new livery features blue and red stripes down each side of the fuselage with the words 'Jersey European' in blue.

Late in 1979 Mr Leslie Thomas retired as chairman of Intra. He started out with Jersey Airlines, and then joined BUA(CI). After that airline closed down in 1968, Mr Thomas and others formed Intra. He is carrying on as a consultant to Express Air Services, one of the joint owners of Jersey European.

AIR ECOSSE

Air Ecosse, a subsidiary of Fairflight Charters Ltd of Biggin Hill which started operations in July 1977, ferries men and materials around the North Sea oil fields. Based at Aberdeen's Dyce airport, the charter company provides contract, spot hire or individual passenger or freight transport. A motley assortment of aircraft has been utilised, including Herons and Navajo Chieftains as well as Heralds.

The Heralds were chartered from BAF and Express Air Services. G-BFRJ flew on the Aberdeen-Shannon-Cork service with Air Ecosse titles. First used on this route was BAF's G-APWA on April 3, 1978. Air Ecosse is one of the fastest-growing third level carriers in the UK.

• • •

Another UK airline which has used Heralds is Dan-Air. For example, it chartered Heralds from BIA to operate flights out of Gatwick to compensate for a shortage of HS748 capacity during 1974. Services were those to Berne and Beauvais. HS748 G-AZSU had been leased to Air Botswana via Hawker Siddeley Aviation, while another was leased to the Conoco Oil Co for two years and based at Aberdeen. These two moves caused a temporary capacity shortage for Dan-Air, which filled it with the BIA Heralds and Alidair Viscounts.

In Service: Foreign Operators

NORDAIR/MARITIME CENTRAL AIRWAYS/ EASTERN PROVINCIAL AIRWAYS

Nordair Ltd of Dorval airport, Montreal, had been a wholly owned subsidiary of Maritime Central Airways for some years when two Heralds were ordered jointly by the companies on February 1, 1961. Nordair was established in 1957 by a merger of Mont Laurier Aviation and Boreal Airways, in which MCA had a controlling interest. In 1958 MCA turned over its substantial Montreal operations to Nordair, allowing MCA to concentrate its capacity on Maritime services.

The first Nordair Herald, CF-NAC, was delivered on February 13, 1962, and put into service on the airline's routes. It soon encouraged a 62 per cent rise in traffic. Services were operated between Montreal, Kingston, Toronto, Hamilton, Sarnia and Windsor, with main bases at Montreal and Roberval.

By the time the second Herald, CF-NAF, had been delivered exactly a month later on March 13, 1962, MCA had decided to relinquish control over Nordair, whose motto was 'serves the north'. So Nordair became a separate company and operated both Heralds for a time.

Simultaneously, MCA decided it also needed two Heralds. These were ordered in February 1962 for delivery in 1963. MCA was the first airline to specify the installation of airborne weather radar in their Heralds. With such safety equipment Heralds could take off and safely maintain flight schedules in weather that would ground aricraft not so equipped. The scanner antenna was fitted in the aircraft nose and covered by a hinged, streamlined glass fibre nose cone.

At this time MCA bought both of the Nordair Heralds as well as their routes. MCA was a private venture company which began regular services in 1941 between Charlottetown on Prince Edward Island and Moncton, New Brunswick. It also undertook charter work to various points in Canada.

In 1962 Eastern Provincial Airways, which provided air communications through Labrador and Newfoundland from its main operating base at Gander, arranged to take over the whole of MCA. This came into force in May 1963.

EPA itself had already ordered and received two Heralds, so the outstanding MCA order was cancelled by arrangement with Handley Page. The first aircraft destined for MCA, CF-MCK, was accordingly repainted for Cruz Airways as PI-C-910. It had appeared in MCA colours at the Farnborough air show in September 1962. The second, CF-MCM, became Globe Air's first Herald (HB-AAG).

EPA had ordered its two Heralds in the same month that Nordair received its first Herald (February 1962). On announcing the order, EPA president Mr Chesley A. Crosbie said: 'This Herald order follows a full examination of all prop-jet aircraft available throughout the world. Our operations demand an aircraft which can land and take-off with ease from a chain of small airfields. It must be economic to run, simple to maintain and provide a very high standard of comfort for passengers.

'In the Herald we shall have an up-to-the-minute aircraft which adequately satisfies all these requirements.'

At this time, EPA was flying services to many points served by Nordair or the latter's parent company, MCA. It was therefore natural that EPA should take over MCA in May 1962.

EPA 'bush' operations played an important part in breaking down the barriers of isolation in Newfoundland by operating winter mail flights and air ambulance services as well as thousands of charter flights. The airline was originally formed in 1949 following a reorganisation of Newfoundland Aero Sales and Services of St John's, with scheduled operations beginning in 1950. Its current name is Eastern Provincial Airways (1963) Ltd.

EPA acquired the two Nordair aircraft to add to its own two, which were delivered in early 1963. The first, CF-EPI, was flown to Canada by an EPA crew, Capt B. Clacken and Capt M. Jones, on February 13, 1963, flying from Radlett via Prestwick, Keflavik, Sondestrom and Frobisher to Gander. It was followed on March 30 by CF-EPC, piloted by Capt Roy Cooper, the airline's chief bushline pilot, and Capt Ben Rivard. Both aircraft flew via the Great Circle route, meaning that no long-range tanks were needed.

Herald CF-EPC touched down at Gander just over 17hr flying time after leaving England, having flown a total distance of 3,272 n.m. No oil had been used during the flight. So little of Keflavik's runway 12 was used when CF-EPC landed that it took a good ten minutes taxiing to reach the terminal building.

When CF-EPC reached Gander, the crew learnt that its sister ship had already notched up 150hr training and proving flying in only 26 days, meaning Herald services could be started as planned.

Following a redefinition of the regional carrier's role in August 1969, the airline's routes now cover services from Montreal to Charlottetown, Halifax, Deer Lake, Stephenville, St John's, Wabush, Churchill/Twin Falls, Goose Bay, Gander, Sydney, Moncton, Chatham, Charlo, Fredericton, Saint John, the Magadalen Islands and St Anthony in the Quebec and Atlantic provinces.

EPA's three remaining Heralds (CF-NAF having been written off on March 17, 1965) were sold to British Air Ferries in 1975.

The Canadian Heralds had to operate in particularly hard conditions, especially in winter when snow or ice covered runways which had strong cross winds. Temperatures dropped to many degrees below zero, and alternate airfields were often many miles away. The Heralds not only operated on inter-city networks in Eastern Canada, but provided air services for Canada's barren eastern arctic regions. They served as a bushline carrying mail, flying doctors and spotting fires with excellent reliability, and proved beyond doubt they were the right airliners for such exacting operations. The low-pressure double-wheeled undercarriage proved its worth during take-offs and landings in the deeply rutted snow of outback landing strips and on short, unmade dirt and stone-covered runways.

EPA's two Heralds, delivered in early 1963, were immediately flown on proving flights to destinations selected by the airline's operations department as proposed scheduled runs. Proving flights of a deliberately realistic nature, carrying both passengers and freight, were made throughout EPA's network from St John's in the south-east corner of Newfoundland to Wabush in north-west Labrador during April 1963. By mid-April the two Heralds had begun scheduled services, and almost immediately the passenger appeal of the type was manifested by increased bookings, accompanied by a marked preference for Heralds over the Dakotas and C-46s flown previously.

Initially, flights were made from Gander to Wabush and Gander to St John's. On the former sector passengers were mostly miners flying (some for the first time) north to Wabush to begin contracts. Businessmen were the usual passengers from Gander to St John's, a trip which took little more than half an hour. On return trips to Gander, Heralds carried much freight and stores, particularly to supply the working parties at Wabush. When they had been operating scheduled services for two or three weeks, a new timetable was devised for them by EPA, based upon the airliner's performance and serviceability.

During 1963 EPA brought about a dramatic increase in its size and sphere of operations by the acquisition of MCA. Even though the two airline's route systems slightly overlapped, this was not to their detriment, since the time schedules were entirely different.

Basically there were two separate networks taken over from MCA and operated by the former company's two Heralds. The first, known as the Maritime schedule, was from New Brunswick to Nova Scotia, from Moncton via Summerside and Charlottetown, House Harbour, New Glasgow and through to Halifax international airport. EPA's northern schedule, taken over from MCA, also started from Moncton, but was routed through Stephenville, Sept Isles, Goose Bay, and thence to Gander and St John's.

AEROLINEE ITAVIA

Aerolinee Itavia was formed in April 1958 and started operations in July 1959. Services had been suspended in 1961, but were restarted again in May 1962 following reorganisation. It was in September 1961 Itavia ordered its first two Heralds, with an option on a third. The first two were handed over in 1963 in part exchange for some of the airline's older Heron aircraft. Itavia, at the time the only Italian independent authorised to operate scheduled services, ordered the Heralds to replace the DC-3s after demonstration flights by G-ARTC in MCA colours over Itavia routes.

Itavia's first example was I-TIVA (originally G-ASBG), delivered on April 12, 1963. It undertook tropical trials at Kano, Nigeria, during February to March, in full Itavia colours. The Herald served for more than ten years before being sold to BIA as G-ASBG in July 1973.

I-TIVE was delivered on May 4, 1963, followed by I-TIVU just over a year later on May 29, 1964. This Herald was also sold to BIA, becoming G-BBXI in December 1973. The last Itavia Herald, I-TIVI, arrived on July 4, 1968, being the penultimate Herald delivered. It, too, came to BIA in 1973 as G-BBXJ.

In addition, the Italian airline also operated G-AVPN on lease from Handley Page from 1967. It was re-registered I-TIVB until it went to BIA in 1973, when it reverted to its original registration.

Initially, Itavia used its Heralds for charters throughout Europe and the Mediterranean regions, eventually placing them on Italian domestic routes from Rome, which this operator did so much to stimulate. But the company had mixed fortunes. It struggled for many years to gain Government subsidies and rent-free premises for its internal services.

Itavia effectively ceased operations in February 1965. That year Dr Aldo Davanzali became the major shareholder, and he is the current president and managing director. Four F-28s were bought to replace the Herald fleet.

GLOBE AIR

Globe Air was a Swiss independent charter operation, registered in 1957, which started operations late in 1960 with an ex-BEA Ambassador. Shortly afterwards the airline looked at several types to replace the ageing Ambassador fleet which it had then built up. By September 1962 the Herald Series 200 had been chosen, as it just fitted the bill. The initial order for two in November 1962 was later

HB-AAG (c/n 162) *Herald of Bern* in flight. (Handley Page)

increased by two repeat orders, bringing the Herald fleet to four with one on option.

Globe Air's 50-seat Heralds were employed on long-term contract and tour charter work to Italy, Mediterranean resorts, North Africa, the Middle East and as far away as Norway.

The first Herald, HB-AAG *Herald of Bern*, was delivered on May 4, 1963, followed by HB-AAH, *Herald of Zurich*, on August 16. Next to arrive was HB-AAK, *Herald of Basle*, on March 13, 1964. The fourth, HB-AAL, *Herald of Interlaken*, was delivered on May 18, 1965. Globe Air placed options on three of the proposed Series 700 aircraft at the end of 1965 because of the success of its Heralds.

After only one year of Herald operations, the airline returned some remarkable operational statistics. These included a peak utilisation of up to 18hr per day during summer weekends, an average load factor of 98 per cent, and less than six mechanical faults of a minor nature. Even more noteworthy was the fact that routine servicing and maintenance was done in the open – Globe Air had no hangarage, and fewer personnel to keep their Heralds airborne than many similar operators.

Palma was the main destination (on peak weekends Heralds made three return trips per day), and points of departure were mostly Berne, Zurich, Geneva, Basle and Gatwick. The Canary Islands, Malaga, Valencia, Venice and Dubrovnik were frequently visited. Contract charter was undertaken carrying students to Tel Aviv via Nicosia, and flights to the northern hemisphere often included Bardufoss in Norway. In winter, 42-seater Safari flights were flown fortnightly to Nairobi via Brindisi, Athens, Cairo, Khartoum, Juba and Entebbe.

Globe Air operated almost entirely for the benefit of holiday-makers and tourists. Such was the frequency of flights that they could almost have been regarded as regular. The main season was from June to September, when flying was broken down to 40 per cent to and from Palma, 50 per cent to other holiday destinations and 10 per cent *ad hoc* charter work.

High aircraft utilisation made it impossible for the carrier to accept freight contracts, but, specialised freight was occasionally carried. In 1963, for example, about ten flights were made from Bremen to Madrid, each carrying 30,000 to 40,000 chicks.

Sometimes the Heralds met quite severe weather conditions, with heavy hail in the Basle area as well as gusty weather southwards in the more mountainous regions around Berne and Zurich.

One optional extra fitted was a moveable cabin bulkhead. Although Globe Air Heralds were equipped as one class airliners, the bulkhead could provide a separate first class cabin if required.

Unfortunately, a trail of trouble followed in the wake of the airline's Britannia disaster near Nicosia in April 1967, when 117 passengers and nine crew died, and Globe Air petitioned to be wound up on October 17 that year. The next day the Swiss Federal Aviation Office announced it had grounded the airline's remaining fleet of two Heralds and one Britannia.

ARKIA - ISRAEL INLAND AIRLINES

Arkia, Israel's internal airline, was founded jointly in January 1950 by El Al and Histadrut, the General Federation of Labour, on the initiative of the then Minister of Transport David Remez. The responsibility of managing the new company was given to Jacob Hozman, who remained at its head until his death in 1965. His great drive and energy helped enormously to make Arkia ('I will soar') the successful enterprise it is today, employing nearly 400 people.

In the early 1960s an order for three Fokker F-27s was contemplated, but Arkia finally plumped for five Heralds instead. It initially ordered two of the type in November 1963 to help expand its domestic and charter operations. Although the F-27 was faster, the Herald could fly more passengers, and was therefore chosen.

The familiar whine of the Herald inaugurated jet age internal air travel in Israel. Arkia provides the only fast link between Eilat, the Red Sea 'honeymoon town' holiday resort, and Tel Aviv in the north of the country. Tourists, convalescents and Israeli nationals form the bulk of traffic on this 55min flight.

It was announced in August 1965 a third Herald would be bought, while a fourth was ordered in January 1968. 4X-AHS was delivered to Arkia on May 18, 1964, arriving at Tel Aviv a month after 4X-AHR, which had arrived on April 17. 4X-AHR was sold to BIA in 1973 as G-BAZJ.

Next to be delivered was 4X-AHT on July 28, 1966, followed by 4X-AHO on April 10, 1968 and 4X-AHN, the last Herald built, on August 15, 1968. They formed the backbone of Israel's domestic air communications network. Arkia's

Arkia Herald 4X-AHT (c/n 189) (APN)

managing director, Mr Lev Bigon, took delivery of 4X-AHO at Radlett. The order was worth more than £330,000 – quite a jump from the original Herald price. This aircraft joined the other three on scheduled routes between Tel Aviv and such places as Eilat, Jerusalem, Rosh-Pina and the Dead Sea airport of Massada, 1,290ft below sea level, and also took its turn on the Tel-Aviv-Nicosia Herald services, chartered from Arkia by El Al.

The 'lowest point on earth' – the Dead Sea region – was served by the four remaining Heralds, using the strip at Massadah to disembark tourists and invalids visiting the nearby mineral springs and rest homes. The Heralds were also used for many educational aerial trips around Israel. Arkia offers a range of flights for children and students of varying ages. Much interest is shown in these trips mainly by educational bodies who want to combine a study of the country with flights over the territories.

For the convenience of passengers, and to avoid having to drive out to Lod international airport, Arkia sited its home base at Tel Aviv. Here, at Sde Dov airport, ten minutes from the city centre, the airline set up its technical installations. Having the airport so near to a heavily built-up area has been a factor in the steady growth of internal air passenger traffic in the country. In 1964, the year the first Herald arrived, the airline carried 154,000 passengers. By 1965 the figure had risen to 180,622. Arkia carried around 700,000 passengers a year with its fleet of Heralds and Viscounts in the mid-1970s.

After the 1967 Arab-Israeli Six Day War (the reason 4X-AHO went to Israel, where it was needed to boost the fleet now flying on new routes because of the conflict), a daily sight-seeing tour of the country's newly held territory was started. They were booked weeks in advance, proving extremely popular with nationals and foreign tourists alike.

Starting at Tel Aviv, the Herald tours took in low-level aerial views of the Gaza coast, Mitla Pass, Mount Sinai and the famous monastery of Santa Catherina, Sharm-el-Sheikh (strategically important, as it is at the tip of the Sinai Peninsula and commands the entrance to the Gulf of Eilat), Ras Nasrani and the Tiran Straits before landing at Eilat. After lunch and a swim in the Red Sea, passengers took off again to look down upon the Dead Sea, Massadah, Jericho, Bethlehem, Jerusalem and Ramalla before returning to Tel Aviv. Altogether, the round trip took about seven hours and light refreshments were served during the flight.

KANAF-ARKIA

In 1972 Arkia acquired a 50 per cent holding in the third level and charter airline, Kanaf-Arkia. This move gave El Al a granddaughter! Currently flying Britten-Norman Islanders, some scheduled services are operated for Arkia as the 'mother' airline.

• • •

With the coming of the Heralds, the financial position of Arkia improved in 1965. The first two Heralds, delivered in mid-1964, gave the airline an extra 36 per cent capacity. In 1965 Herald utilisation rose from 3.3hr per day to 5.8hr.

During the June 1967 war, the three Heralds were attached to the Air Force and did their bit evacuating the wounded, along with Dakotas. The planes operated on a 24hr basis without lights or proper navigational equipment. A great upswing in traffic after the Six Day War resulted in the fourth and fifth Heralds for Arkia, which leased a Bavaria Herald to cope with demand until their extra aircraft were delivered.

A sixth Herald would probably have been ordered, but the collapse of Handley Page put an end to such plans. Indeed, Arkia found the Herald so suitable that 12 may have been in service by 1975.

By 1976 Arkia started to evaluate the Boeing 737-200, DC-9 30/40 and One-Eleven Series 500 for its future jet equipment. Bigon opted for the One-Eleven, and financial problems resulted in the phasing out of the Heralds in 1977/78 (*see* Express Air Freight).

ALIA - ROYAL JORDANIAN AIRLINES

Alia is a wholly Government-owned national airline, established on December 4, 1963, to succeed Jordan Airways. Its formation was personally ordered by King Hussein. In the same month the two Heralds with the Royal Jordanian Air Force were transferred to Alia and placed on internal routes, in particular on the tourist run to Aqaba. They also flew sectors such as Amman-Jerusalem, Beirut-Cairo and Kuwait. Scheduled services started only 11 days after the airline had been formed.

No special modifications to the Heralds were needed, although they could be quickly prepared for the military role if the occasion arose. At the outset load factors averaged 65 per cent, with a daily utilisation of 6.7hr. In six months load factors were touching 100 per cent. Complete turn-round times averaged 15min, and in one two-day period Alia flew no fewer than 1,400 passengers between Cairo and Amman with no technical troubles. Shortest stage length was from Amman to Jerusalem - just 12min.

G-ASPJ (c/n 173) was given this registration for lease to Alia from February until March 10, 1964. It went to Globe-Air on March 13 that year.

Tragedy struck the airline on April 10, 1965, when JY-ACQ met a disastrous fate. Explosive decompression and a major structural failure led to a crash at Demas, which killed 45 on board. At that time the aeroplane had flown 1,500hr and made 1,450 landings.

To demonstrate his faith in the Herald after the crash, King Hussein, a qualified Herald pilot and a regular customer of the airline, asked the Prime Minister and Alia's chief officials to board the other Herald, JY-ACR, and he then flew the aircraft over Amman as a gesture of confidence. It was subsequently put up for sale, as Jerusalem airport was closed for enlargement at the time, and the airline's new Caravelles had enough capacity to meet all obligations on scheduled and IT services.

BAVARIA FLUG-GESELLSCHAFT

Bavaria of Munich, one of Germany's leading charter airlines, used to fly cargo services for Deutsche Lufthansa between Hamburg, Bremen, Hanover and Frankfurt using ex-Lufthansa DC-3s. In November 1963 founder-director Max Schwabe began negotiations with Handley Page to buy Heralds, and returned to England on January 28, 1964, to sign a contract for one aircraft with two more on option.

Using just one Herald D-BIBI delivered on May 1, 1964, Bavaria carried more than 12,000 tourists that year alone. During the following two years the airline sold two of its executive aircraft and took delivery of two more Heralds. D-BEBE *Herald of Bavaria* was delivered on March 29, 1965, and D-BOBO *Herald of the Alps* arrived on April 4, 1966.

The inclusive tour routes flown extended to North Africa, the Balkans, Italy and Spain. In 1966 Bavaria's aircraft logged nearly 8,000 flying hours and carried some 80,000 passengers and 4,000 tons of freight.

With the introduction of a second BAC 1-11 414 into service in the spring of 1968, the Heralds were relegated to cargo work. Bavaria also used its Heralds on early morning newspaper flights from Munich-Milan and Munich-Hamburg-Venice.

To overcome the big handicap of the IT business – the drop-off of passengers in winter – Bavaria took over scheduled routes on sub-charter from leading airlines and managed to secure charter contracts from the Israeli airline Arkia, another Herald operator. These scheduled flights within Israel were made by 50-seat Heralds with German aircrews and Israeli cabin staff.

D-BEBE was leased to Arkia on November 24, 1967, and withdrawn from service in 1970. It was delivered to BIA as G-AYMG on November 13, 1970. D-BOBO was returned to Handley Page as G-ATHE on October 14, 1968, and D-BIBI was sold to Handley Page on June 22, 1967, as G-AVPN.

BAHAMAS AIRWAYS

Bahamas Airways was founded in 1936 to take over the operation of inter-island charter services, which began in 1933. The Herald had a fleeting romance with Bahamas Airways for a few months in 1964. The Eastern Provincial Herald CF-EPC was leased to this operator as VP-BCG from February until May, but it is not known whether the aircraft was painted in the airline's livery.

SADIA/TRANSBRASIL

Sadia SA Transportes Aereos was formed in São Paulo in 1955 to carry meat products for the Sadia organisation. This Brazilian domestic airline began scheduled passenger services the following March and flew to points in the south-east and north-east of the country.

In 1962 Sadia chose the Dart Herald for its expanding network to help reduce losses. It seemed that only one Brazilian operator was convinced that an aircraft like the Herald could replace the DC-3 on domestic routes and make more money. So Sadia began negotiating for five Heralds, and a seemingly endless process of form-filling, obtaining permission from the President of Brazil downwards, collecting signatures and waiting was set in motion.

The greatest obstacle the airline faced was the formalities governing the import of foreign aircraft and spare parts into Brazil. It held up the signing of the order until January 6, 1965. The three-year-long story could probably fill a very large book in itself. Omar Fontana, Sadia's president, travelled between his office at São Paulo's Congonhas airport and Rio de Janeiro about 300 times, all told, collecting various signatures.

The order was a big breakthrough for Handley Page in the lucrative South American market. It followed one of the most intensive and competitive sales battles ever staged in the 'DC-3 replacement' arena, with the F-27 and Hawker Siddeley 748 as the Herald's main opponents. Handley Page estimated there was a market for 400 Heralds in Latin America – for there were about that number of elderly aircraft in service in that part of the world.

As soon as it was made known that Sadia had a marked preference for the Herald, Handley Page made two available under lease agreement from January 1964 to enable the airline to make a practical examination of performance, engineering and operating costs. Both aircraft were in passenger-carrying service on Brazilian routes for several months. Subsequently Dr Fontana, a qualified lawyer who has always expressed unbounded enthusiasm for the Dart Herald, said: 'We have made an intensive operational evaluation of the Herald which has convinced us that it is the finest aircraft in its class. Reliability has been excellent and Handley Page service has been outstandingly good. No other competitive aeroplane can carry 50 passengers and 2,000lb of cargo over this stage length', he added, referring to the 595-mile Rio de Janeiro-Brasilia sector. Most of the airline's average stage lengths were 180 miles.

'With its gluttony for hard work, lower operating costs and longer overhaul life than any comparable airliner, the Herald has conclusively proved again its superiority and effectiveness on regional services', said the manufacturers after winning the £1,500,000 contract.

Fontana gave the Brazilian Director of Civil Aviation the following reasons for choosing the Herald:

1. Better take-off and landing performance on rough fields.
2. Greater passenger and cargo capacity.
3. Larger access doors to the holds and a fuselage closer to the ground to facilitate loading.
4. Able to ground start without need of ground generators (which would have cost the airline another $6,500).
5. Operational and maintenance simplicity.

Sadia started using Heralds on its ex-DC-3 routes from February 1964, and passenger traffic and load factors built up quickly. By the end of that year two Heralds were in constant use; by the end of 1965 there were four; and by early 1966 all five were in operation. They were changed from 50- to 46-seaters to give more leg room. In early 1966 Sadia was seeking to buy three more Heralds, as well as negotiating for three BAC 1-11s, because the new traffic being generated suggested that the three additional Heralds would be needed for 1966-67. In fact, only one more was to arrive (PP-SDN, in January 1968).

Sadia has expanded continuously since its formation in 1955. Products from the meat packing factory, SA Industria e Comercio Concordia, started by Omar's father, bore the brand name 'Sadia' – from the first two and last three letters of the registered name, which in Portuguese means 'healthy'. So the airline was a 'healthy' advertisement for the business.

Some remarkable statistics were revealed by Dr Fontana covering his 1964 operations with the Heralds. In that year the total operating cost per seat-km for each Herald, including depreciation, amounted to only a little more than it did for the airline's Dakotas.

Sadia and VASP both operated the highly-competitive Ponte Aerea air bridge between São Paulo and Rio, and Fontana nearly always achieved best monthly place in punctual performance.

The first colour scheme consisted of twin medium blue cheat lines with white top decking and white dividing line. The front of the fin was blue, as was the insignia on the tail. 'Sadia', with the S and the dot of the 'i' in red, originally appeared between the cockpit and the leading edge of the wing as well as on the engine nacelles, but was later repositioned on the rear fuselage. At the same time the scheme was changed to dark green and gold, with a sun-type motif on the fin. PP-SDJ was the first to appear in this country in full Sadia livery. Before that aircraft had been delivered to Brazil devoid of company insignia.

In 1972 the airline changed its name to TransBrasil S/A Linhas Aereas, by which it is now known. In the middle of 1976 the three remaining Heralds with TransBrasil (the other three went to BMA in 1973) were delivered to BAF at Southend prior to going into service with the airline.

Earlier in 1976 Brazil's civil aviation board (DCA) had announced that it was creating five third-level carriers to improve air links inside the country. At the time only 72 Brazilian cities could boast that they had an airline service. DCA aimed to raise this number to 200 by 1977, and to 400 by 1980.

Transportes Aereos Bacia Amazonica (TABA), which leased all three of TransBrasil's Heralds in 1975-76, uses Bandeirantes and other smaller twins to improve services in the northern part of the country, where it has been operating for 15 years.

The Heralds were used on routes in the Amazonas region carrying TABA-NOTA titles, 'NOTA' being Norte Taxi Aereo, which merged with TABA.

G-ASKK (c/n 161) was leased as PP-ASU for nine months from December 6, 1963, becoming the first Herald to be operated by Sadia. It went back to BMA in early 1965.

G-APWA (c/n 149) was leased as PP-ASV from February 20, 1964, (having left Luton for Brazil on February 15) until October 24, 1965. It returned to Sadia as PP-SDM on November 18, 1966, and stayed until it was sold to BAF in 1976.

PP-SDG (c/n 185) first flew as G-8-3 and was delivered on October 6, 1964, after appearing at Farnborough in September as G-ASVO in Sadia colours. It came to BMA in March 1973 as G-ASVO.

PP-SDH (c/n 186) was delivered on January 26, 1965. It was sold to BAF as G-BEBB, arriving at Southend on July 15, 1976.

G-ATIG (c/n 177) was sold to Sadia as PP-SDI on September 18, 1965. It came to BMA in April 1973.

PP-SDJ (c/n 190) was delivered on December 7, 1965. It was the only Brazilian Herald to be written off, after crashing on Marumbi Peak, Curitiba on November 3, 1967, killing 16 passengers and five crew.

PP-SDL (c/n 191) was delivered in February 1966. It left Radlett for Luton under the command of Capt E. R. Silva. PP-SDL left Prestiwck on February 2 for the ocean crossing. It was sold to BAF as G-BDZV and delivered on June 30, 1976.

PP-SDN (c/n 194) was delivered on January 10, 1968. It came to BMA in April 1973 as G-BAVX.

G-AVEZ (c/n 169) was leased from January 13, 1968, as PP-ASW. It went back to BU(CI)A on April 9, 1968.

FAR EASTERN AIR TRANSPORT

Far Eastern Air Transport's first Herald, B-2001 (c/n 162) seen shortly after delivery to the Taiwan airline. (Handley Page)

Far Eastern Air Transport was formed in 1957 by a former CAT pilot and his brother, who became chairman. The airline, based at Taipei in Formosa, ordered two Heralds in June 1965, giving Handley Page a foothold in the American-dominated Far Eastern market. They were the first turboprops to be placed on scheduled services in Taiwan, and were also the first British-built aircraft to be operated there.

The Heralds replaced the airline's fleet of C-45s, and complemented FAT's cargo-carrying DC-3s, being used initially to develop the Taipei-Kaohsiung, Tainan, Hualien and Makung Island routes.

B-2001 was delivered on February 16, 1966, after having previously been returned to Handley Page as G-ATHB. It was formerly Globe Air's HB-AAG. The aircraft was originally to have been delivered in the autumn.

FAT was another airline to tragically lose a Herald. A Whisky series aircraft, ex-BU(CI)A G-APWI, was sold at the end of 1968 to FAT as B-2009. It was written off on February 24, 1969, after it made a forced landing and struck a ditch shortly after take-off from Kaohsiung at Cheluchien, Southern Taiwan. There was an engine fire and 36 people were killed.

Just five days earlier a third Herald, B-2011, was sold to the airline. Colour scheme was a red cheat line and fin flash, FAT in white and Herald titling and registration in black. B-2001, which operated three services a day each way on the main route between Taipei and the seaport of Kaohsiung, carried the Formosan flag on the fin as well as the registration. B-2001 and B-2011 were engineless in Taiwan in 1975.

AIR MANILA

Air Manila started operations in January 1965, and served a number of commercial and tourist points throughout the Philippine islands. Formed the previous February by local business interests, it was licensed to operate by the Civil Aeronautics Board in March 1964, using DC-3s on the money-making trunkline routes.

The contract for two Heralds signed by the airline in 1965, followed close on the heels of another from Asia – that of the order placed by Far Eastern Air Transport of Taiwan. Total value of both orders plus spares was £1½ million.

First to arrive in the Philippines was PI-C866 (c/n 192), delivered from Radlett on March 18, 1966, via Luton and Marseilles.

G-ASBP (c/n 163) was the former BUA executive aircraft, and appeared at the Farnborough air show in September 1966 in Air Manila colours. It was leased to the airline in March for two months before delivery on October 21, 1966, as PI-C869.

For centuries Filipinos relied on colourful sailing vintas to maintain communications between their islands. The coming of the go-anywhere Herald revolutionised the scene. Air Manila introduced the type on its inter-island services and Heralds operated their island-hopping services for many years. Those with eagle eyes would have seen the legend 'The Vinta of the Sky' painted in small type on the plane's tail fin.

G-ASBP (c/n 163) appeared at the 1966 Farnborough air show wearing Air Manila livery prior to delivery as PI-C869 that October. (APN)

In February 1966 Air Manila and Filipinas Orient Airways forced Philippine Airlines (PAL) to discontinue its 'Maya' services, a non-scheduled operation started to fight the low fares offered by another operator, FAST.

Air Manila ceased operations from August to December 1969 because of a scarcity of pilots and aircraft. Losses, debts, cancellations and grounded aircraft among the airlines in the Philippines led to a Senate investigation. Martial law was declared in September 1972, and the Air Force took over the operations of the airlines.

In March 1973 President Marcos designated PAL the sole Philippine flag carrier (starting from January 1974). FOA and Air Manila could not agree on plans to integrate, so their operations were shut down in December 1973. They were absorbed on January 2, 1974, by PAL and the services and staff of all three airlines integrated into one operation. Discussions regarding a merger had been under way since 1969, but heavy financial losses in 1973 accelerated the private airlines' demise.

But there was life in Air Manila yet. The airline started up charter flights in 1974, as that was better than nothing at all. Permission was granted in March that year, and in December the licence was extended to take in international flights, so the operator added 'International' to its name.

Since the transfer of Air Manila's 17-point domestic network to PAL in January 1974, the sole Herald has been used on domestic and regional charter work.

Not surprisingly, Air Manila's history has not run smoothly over the years, but signs suggest that the going is improving, and the airline would like to operate scheduled domestic services once again. Accidents have been numerous – ten on the ground and in the air, and Air Manila lost seven aircraft (including a Herald) in the 1970 typhoon.

Operations were grounded by the Philippine government following the loss of Electra RP-C1061 at Guam on June 4, 1976, when the aeroplane crashed on take-off and all the 45 people aboard lost their lives. Two months later, after an airworthiness check, flying was resumed.

Up to February 29, 1976, Herald RP-C866 had flown 11,626hr and made only 9,365 landings – virtually the lowest of all civilian Heralds. By May 1978 the Herald had clocked up 12,388hr and 10,213 landings, but during the year RP-C866 is thought to have been withdrawn from use.

EUROPE AERO SERVICE

Europe Aero Service was formed in 1965 as a subsidiary of Société Aero Sahara. Scheduled passenger services began in 1966 from the airline's base at Perpignan in France, and now operate Paris (Orly)-Valence, Nimes-Palma and Perpignan-Lyon.

In 1968 the operator took delivery of two Heralds, both part of the former Globe Air fleet which was grounded the previous October. The Heralds operated short-haul routes to Geneva, Ajaccio and Bastia, as well as doing general charter work.

F-OCLY was delivered to Globe Air as HB-AAK and was re-registered F-BLOY. F-OCLZ was delivered to the Swiss operator as HB-AAL. It is currently registered F-BOIZ. Both are still operated by EAS.

The original Herald colour scheme included the registration on the fin band, but a slight redesigning resulted in the registration being placed above the cheat line on the rear fuselage and EAS appearing in white on the blue fin band outlined in white.

While one Herald was kept for *ad hoc* charters, the other was used on the important Valence-Paris route. Heralds started operating this sector in June 1969, with EAS offering two round trips per day, five days per week.

In the mid-1960s, the main source of income for Société Aero Sahara was charter work connected with oil-drilling operations. In December 1965 it was awarded a licence under the name of Europe Aero Service for scheduled third level services. EAS is probably best known as the airline that has seen more Vickers Vanguards pass through its hands than any other operator.

LINEAS AEREAS LA URRACA

Lineas Aereas La Urraca was formed in January 1963 by the Henao-Jaramillo brothers. Scheduled services are operated from Bogota and Villavicencio to points in the south of Colombia, together with domestic charters.

Urraca bought the three ex-Autair Heralds (G-APWB, 'WC and 'ED) in 1970. They were overhauled by Field Aircraft Services and then flown to Colombia via Prestwick, after being placed in open storage at Castle Donington. *Whisky Bravo* became HK-718, *Whisky Charlie* HK-715 *Bochica* and

Whisky Delta HK-721, and all three were based at Villavicencio.

Unfortunately, the Heralds have suffered an unhappy time in South America. All three have been involved in accidents (q.v.), and only HK-715 is reported to be still in service. In December 1977 this aircraft was seen at Villavicencio under re-build and completely silver in appearance, presumably stripped down to bare metal.

The airline's owners are Capt Alvaro Henao-Jaramillo (one of the founder members) and Mrs Nydia Quintero de Henao.

An interesting footnote: all Colombian civil aircraft have to carry the Colombian merchant flag, and airlines must have the word 'Colombia' painted on their planes after the company name.

NILE VALLEY AVIATION

Nile Valley Aviation is a new Egyptian company originally formed as an air taxi, charter and aerial survey operator. It began scheduled passenger services between Cairo and Alexandria in 1977 - the first such services for ten years. These were suspended, however, after the owner's death in July 1977.

Nile Valley also undertakes photographic work and supply services to petroleum companies. Heralds have been leased from BAF, including G-BAVX, G-BEYE and G-BEYD, normally for a few months at a time. Nile Valley also provides tourist charters for tour operators to well-known attractions in Egypt.

GULF AIR

Gulf Air of Bahrain has leased various Heralds from BAF over the past few years, including G-ASVO and G-BEYF.

G-BAVX on lease to Nile Valley Aviation. c/n is 194. (S. Piercey)

STYRIA AIRLINES

Styria Airlines, originally named Syrian Airlines, leased a Herald from Itavia for operation from the Austrian county of Steiermark on daily services Graz Klagenfurt-Innsbruck-Frankfurt, carrying green and white Steiermark colours. Services were supposed to start on April 1, 1970. The company was formed on February 28 that year in Austria by the county of Steiermark and Itavia.

ROUSSEAU AVIATION

It was reported Rousseau Aviation operated a Herald on lease in 1970.

Military Herald and other Variants

With Malaya's independence in 1957 came a need for the country to form its own air force to perform the important task of aerial communication. This work, together with offensive duties during the country's guerilla emergency, had previously been carried out almost entirely by units of the Royal Air Force deployed from the UK. On June 2, 1958, the Royal Malayan Air Force came into being, made up of seconded RAF officers and N.C.Os and a small number of Malayan airmen transferred from the RAF (Malaya) and RAF Regiment (Malaya).

The years 1959 and 1960 were spent in training pilots and ground-crews. It was then decided to expand the RMAF to a sufficient extent to allow it to take over most of the RAF's commitments in the country. When Malaysia was first mooted, the RMAF realised that its responsibilities in the resulting Federation (formed on September 16, 1963) could not be discharged with its current fleet, as it would have to move large numbers of troops and supplies over fairly long distances. Thus the RMAF decided to purchase eight Heralds, along with Alouette helicopters and two Herons.

By comparison with neighbouring countries, most airfields in Malaysia were of a very high standard, being well paved and of adequate length. This was because most towns served by air, as well as some of the larger centres for rubber and tin production, had their airstrips developed in the late 'fifties and early 'sixties to accept F-27s operated by Malayan Airways.

Future Herald flight crews were drawn from the cream of Twin Pioneer captains after they completed some 1,200hr flying time as first pilots. Until the Heralds were delivered, Twin Pioneers were the largest STOL transports to have served with the RMAF.

The late morning of November 8, 1963, was fine and cloudless when FM1020, the first Herald Series 401 for the Royal Malaysian Air Force, landed at Kuala Lumpur. A large welcoming party, headed by base commander Wg Cdr G. Frain, greeted the men who had ferried the plane out from the UK, Officer Commanding Sqn Ldr D. R. Bryan, the Flight Commander Flt Lt Norman Rose and Flt Off B. H. Love.

Flt Lt Rose was seconded to the RMAF from 1963 and 'grew up' with the Heralds. FM1020 was in the final stages of construction, and he ferried it out to Malaysia after a conversion course on the type. The crew had completed courses of instruction at the Rolls-Royce and Handley Page Schools (Derby and Radlett), and had undergone about ten hours conversion flying with Jersey Airlines in October 1963.

FM1020 had flown out from Luton on November 2, and arrived at Kuala Lumpur six days later. Familiarisation and working-up took place in November and December, including STOL trials at Taiping. Flt Lt Rose wrote the pilots' notes and operation procedures for the Herald in military service.

While FM1020 was given an acceptance check, the aircrew set off in G-APWA (in Malaysia on temporary loan) on a 25hr training programme to visit most of the airfields in West and East Malaysia to assess their suitability for Herald operations.

The Herald was then the fastest, biggest and largest load-carrying aircraft in the RMAF. It could carry 50 troops, 24 casualty stretchers or a 10,000lb freight load. The eight machines ordered joined No 4 Squadron, based at Kuala Lumpur. Scheduled route flying to East Malaysia also began in December, flying from Kuala Lumpur to Changi, Kuching, Labuan, Jesselton and Tawau.

On December 31, 1963, Flt Lt Rose had to fly eight dead soldiers, the first victims of 'confrontation' with neighbouring Indonesia, from Tawau to Kuala Lumpur. Unfortunately, the corpses were not put in coffins. 'The smell was indescribable', he recalled. 'They were not boxed or sealed. Just white sheets covered in blood were put over them. They had been dead for several days, so you can imagine the state they were in.'

After the four and a half hour flight, which came to be known by pilots as 'body vacs', the plane was met by Prime Minister Tunku Abdul Rahman. Later, 'body vac' corpses were sealed in bags.

Herald FM-1022 (c/n 175) at Luton during the winter of 1964/65 ready for delivery to Malaysia. (Philip Birtles)

At the time the Herald was considered a prestige aircraft, and so it was quite natural that VIPs wanted to fly in it. An aircraft could be transformed from a military to a VIP fit in about four hours, and proved popular among dignataries. The first VIP flight of a RMAF Herald took place when the Prime Minister flew to Phnom Penh, Cambodia, to visit Prince Sihanouk on February 10, 1964, in FM1022. On April 10 the same Herald took New Zealand Prime Minister Sir Keith Holyoak from Singapore to Kuala Lumpur, and that same month supply drop trials began.

The squadron quadrupled its strength in aircraft and aircrews in three months after the arrival of the first. FM1021, 1022 and 1023 arrived from the UK at monthly intervals, ferried out by loaned personnel. Aircrews continued to join the unit, four pilots coming from the Royal Australian Air Force and three Malaysian co-pilots coming from other RMAF squadrons.

For the first five months No 4 Squadron flew with only one recognised AQM - Sgt Sen Gupta. Later he was joined by five more Malaysians who had completed their training at Thorney Island. In January 1966 six more Malaysians swelled the ranks to the correct level.

Another 'first' came on May 7, 1964, with the first Royal Flight, from Kuala Lumpur to Singapore. The 13 states comprising Malaysia take it in turns in having a King and Queen of Malaysia. The Malaysian title for King is Yang di Pertuan Agong.

A tragic incident that had a happy ending occurred, when injured soldier 11237 was flown by Flt Lt Rose from Jesselton to Kuala Lumpur, thus saving his life. 'I have often wondered what became of him', said Flt Lt (now Sqn Ldr) Rose. 'I would love to hear from him again.'

November 1965 saw a royal tour of East Malaysia, with Gloster Javelin escorts flying alongside the Herald.

Almost straight after its formation, No 4 Squadron had begun operational flying, a fortnightly three-day schedule to Sarawak and Sabah being initiated. Those early days caused problems, as staging airfields had little technical knowledge of the Herald and spare parts were virtually non-existent. Nonetheless, No 4 slowly and surely began building a reputation for a prompt and efficient air transport service (20min turnrounds, dead on schedule and hardly any unserviceabilities).

High priority was given to training. Captains and co-pilots had to complete three and four hours flying training respectively each month.

In the early days, the Herald was assessed in the SEAC supply dropping role, but it was decided it was not the ideal aircraft for the job. The main trouble was that the Herald could not lose speed and height quickly enough to be at the proper dropping height in the deep valleys of the highlands. When used in the roller conveyor role, 6,000lb of supplies left the aircraft in six seconds!

The eighth and last aircraft was delivered in January 1965, having been ferried out by Sqn Ldr Bryan and Flt Off Poong. However, the squadron was unable to operate all of its aircraft for many months - in fact, it was only in June that all eight were operational. The second batch of four Heralds was fitted

Model of the HP124 Military Herald project. (Handley Page)

with autopilots, inward-opening sliding rear doors and an improved compass display. In early 1965 the first of the original aircraft left for the UK for autopilot installation and compass modification – the sliding doors having been decided against. Pilots demanded that autopilots be fitted to all aircraft, so eventually all eight machines eventually came back to the UK to have them installed. The autopilots were bought from Handley Page.

In April 1965 an offensive operation by night was mounted by Herald FM1027. It involved dropping propaganda leaflets over areas where infiltrators were known to be hiding south east of Singapore.

'We took off from Kuala Lumpur for Changi, where we overshot at 50ft with all lights off', said Flt Lt Rose. 'Then we would fly low-level over the area. We were fired on by Indonesians. I remember seeing pink balls coming up at us. It was pretty scary. That is the only time I recall that a Herald was fired at.'

On January 9, 1966, FM1020 took Edward Heath, Chris Chataway and Anthony Barber from Singapore to Saigon during the Vietnam War. A RAF Britannia had broken down at Changi, and a Herald was employed for the flight. It was the first time the squadron had visited war-torn Vietnam.

In April 1965 all aircraft over 18 months old had been grounded for examination following two recent civilian Herald accidents where structural failure as a result of corrosion in the fuselage was thought to be the cause. A modification to strengthen the fuselage was decided upon, and the Hong Kong Aircraft Corporation was contacted to modify seven of the eight aircraft. FM1020 was already in the UK, and the crew had just arrived to collect the aeroplane when the pressurisation problem arose, so they found themselves with several weeks' unexpected leave.

The first aircraft left for Hong Kong for modification in January 1966. It was routed via Labuan and the Philippines, and was fitted with long-range tanks to allow it to return to the Philippines or divert to Formosa in case of an unexpected deterioration in the weather at Hong Kong.

As one aircraft was modified, the next would depart, and the crew would fly back the modified one. The first return aircraft came direct Hong Kong-Kuala Lumpur (1,430n.m. - 1,650 statute miles), and the last aircraft was completed in August 1966. No corrosion was discovered, but these safety measures were much appreciated by the aircrews.

December 1965 and January 1967 are well remembered for the extensive flooding around the north-east coast of West Malaysia. The squadron mounted airlifts with relief workers, carrying blankets, boats, rice and medical supplies. 'Operation Cold Feet', in December 1965, was carried out in low cloud and constant rain. The atrocious weather made flying difficult, but only one aircraft was forced to divert back to Kuala Lumpur. Four air supply drops were made from Herald aircraft.

The following is a break-down of the two operations:

Passengers	**Air-landed**	**Air-dropped**	**Flights**	**Hours**
Dec 1965 - 278	204,170lb	26,250lb	70	90.25
Jan 1967 - 324	414,524lb	40,395lb	135	176

By March 1966 the squadron had completed its first 10,000hr flying. For the first three years it was manned mostly by personnel loaned by the RAF and RAAF, except for the airmen. On January 1, 1967, Sqn Ldr Welch assumed command to become No 4 Squadron's first Malaysian commander.

Flt Lt Rose spent three years with the squadron as Flight Commander Training Officer, and notched up 2,000hr plus flying. Flt Lt Bernie Donders arrived in August 1967 for a three-year stint as Squadron Qualified Flying Instructor. By that time 'confrontation' with Indonesia had ended.

As was to be expected, the Malaysian Heralds, being military aircraft, were not utilised as intensely as their civilian counterparts. This is confirmed by looking at the number of hours flown and landings made. For instance, the first to be delivered (FM1020 on November 1, 1963) had notched up only 8,733hr and 5,572 landings by May 1976. Others in the squadron had also flown a similar number of hours, the least being 7,585hr and 4,989 landings recorded by FM1027, the last RMAF machine, which had been delivered in January 1965.

Compare this, for example, with the ex-TransBrasil Herald PP-SDH, which was also delivered to its original owner in the same month. Its tally by June 1976 was 23,064hr and 23,809 landings - quite a difference!

The Heralds were phased out during 1976, their place being taken by six Lockheed C-130H Hercules transports.

HERALD VARIANTS

Series 100: The original Dart Herald. A 44-seat version. Maximum AUW was 40,000lb. Powered by Rolls-Royce Dart 7/2 Mark 527 engines. Six built.

Series 200: Designed to improve seat/mile costs by adding an extra 42in to the fuselage as well as increasing take-off weight (to 43,000lb). The definitive version of the Herald. Standard layout was 50 seats at 30.5in pitch. Dart 7/2 power plant of Series 100 kept. Zero fuel weight (ZFW) was 37,000lb and landing weight 39,500lb. Thirty-six built.

Series 300: Identical to Series 200, but modified for the American market. None built.

SERIES 400

The Series 400 was a military freighter equivalent of the Series 200 with side-loading doors and reinforced flooring taking up 200lb/sq ft and fitted with 38 heavy duty lashing points to restrain the load in a 9g acceleration in any direction.

The door surrounds were also strengthened for parachuting, enabling the door to be opened in the air. Special role equipment which could be fitted included a roller conveyor for parachute store dropping, stretcher equipment for the ambulance role, static lines and paratroop seats.

Up to 44 paratroops plus equipment could be carried and dropped in two sticks of 22. The roller conveyor could deal with 32 standard panniers each of 300lb and drop them in a single stick. Dropping speed range was between 95 and 115kt.

The first military Herald delivered was, in fact, not a Series 400 aircraft but a Series 200. 109 (c/n 165) was handed over to the Royal Jordanian Air Force on January 22, 1963, at Radlett airfield. Accepting the aircraft on behalf of King Hussein of Jordan from Mr R. S. Sowter, Handley Page's sales manager, was Brig Mohammed Is-haq, Jordanian military and naval attache in London. He said that the addition of Heralds to the RJAF made possible not only the faster deployment of both troops and equipment within the Middle East, but also the use of hitherto impossible landing strips.

The aircraft was fitted out as a standard 50-seat transport, but its fuselage floor was specially designed to take a roller conveyor with a ball plate platform at the end nearest the aircraft's rear side-loading door. This aeroplane experienced two extremes of temperature within a short time, having been tried and tested for several weeks in the intense cold in England and then having to operate in hot temperatures in Jordan.

Only eight Series 400 were built, all going to the Royal Malaysian Air Force. At the Paris air show in June 1963, Handley Page announced that the RMAF had ordered the second batch of four aircraft. Deliveries of the first Series 400 were to start later in the year.

The Series 400 was evaluated by the RAF against the Avro (later Hawker Siddeley) 748, but although it was found to be superior in almost every respect, the RAF finally placed an order with Hawker Siddeley for the Andover.

In the House of Commons on April 6, 1962, the Parliamentary Secretary to the Ministry of Aviation, Mr C. M. Woodhouse, said the extra development cost for the Dart 12 engine was still being assessed, but was likely to work out at about £5,000 per engine.

'The time scale', he said, 'is that it would need about 18 months for development from the date of contract, but the important point which I wish to emphasise is that the recommendation of the Ministry of Aviation experts was that, whichever of the two aircraft were chosen, the Dart 12 engine would have to be installed if either aircraft were to meet the specification.

'With the Dart 10, the Air Ministry specification would not be fully met. The subsequent cost of stocking and maintaining engines would be substantially the same, whether it was the Dart 10 or the Dart 12, because from the Royal Air Forces's point of view both are new engines.'

Mr Woodhouse added: 'I should like to reiterate, as the Hon Member for Loughborough (Mr Cronin) has very rightly said, that these are both very fine aircraft, and I should like to pay a personal tribute to the technical and engineering skill that has been put into the Herald as well as the Avro 748'.

King Hussein himself completed negotiations for buying the two Heralds for the RJAF in the summer of 1962. Earlier that year he had seen a Herald demonstrated on the soft sand strip at Aqaba on the Red Sea.

The Heralds, resplendent in a red cheat line livery, white top fuselage with the Jordanian flag on the fin and roundels of green, white and black with serial in black on the fuselage, were identical to other Series 200s.

One requirement of the RJAF was the transport of turbo-jet engines for their Hunter jets, weighing 3,500lb each. Using the roller conveyor four men could load or unload one of the heavy Rolls-Royce Avons. Two engines could be transported at a time, still leaving room for some passengers. The Heralds were not utilised as much as anticipated, and were consequently demobilised and transferred to Alia (q.v.).

Series 500: Projected version of the basic Series 200 with a R Da 10 power plants rated at 2,775 s.h.p. plus 740lb jet thrust, reversing propellers and lift dumpers for very short field operations (spoilers ahead of the flaps).

The engines would have increased take-off power by more than 40 per cent over the Series 200. Adaptive braking was to be fitted on main wheels, ensuring optimum braking efficiency under all conditions.

The aim of Series 500 was to carry 7,000lb military load 200 miles, land in 1,100ft from 50ft, take-off again at the same weight in 1,350ft to 50ft and fly 200 miles back to base. Gross weight was 46,000lb, 3,000lb more than the Series 400. Its basic operating weight of 27,170lbs left 18,830lb available for fuel and payload. The increase in power raised estimated cruising speed to 287 m.p.h. for maximum range. None built.

Series 600: Major development of the Series 200. The R Da 7/2 (Mark 527) of Series 200 replaced by R Da 7/H (Mark 532/9) engines, increasing s.h.p. from 1,930 to 2,050. Take-off weight increased to 45,000lb, ZFW to 40,500lb and landing weight to 43,000lb. None built.

Series 700: In 1965 Handley Page announced the Herald 700, planned to replace the Series 200 as the basic model offered for sale. It was claimed it would give even greater scope for airlines to modernise and expand their services economically.

Seating was increased to 60, range upped by 350 miles, and take-off and landing weights increased by 2,000 and 3,500lb. The result, said Handley Page, would be more flexibility for both short and medium haul carriers, and still higher operating profits.

The Herald 700 was due to roll off the production line at Radlett in early 1967, but by 1968 no decision had been taken to go ahead with the more powerful and heavier model because the VASP order for ten aircraft had met with financial troubles.

By March 1966 11 Herald 700s had been ordered by VASP and Far Eastern Air Transport, the Chinese operator based at Taipei, Formosa. Options on three more had been taken by Globe Air of Switzerland. The Herald 700 was to have been powered by Dart 532/9 engines, the maximum take-off weight increased to 45,000lb, the landing weight up to 43,000lb and the zero fuel weight increased by 3,500lb to 40,500lb. Fuel capacity of the outer integral wing tanks was to have been upped by 280gal to give a total capacity of 1,360 Imperial gallons.

A new two-degree take-off flap setting was planned to reduce take-off length at maximum weight, and adaptive braking was to be fitted to shorten landing run. With this system, full braking could be selected before landing so that maximum retardation would come into effect on touchdown. The forward crew door was moved from the port to the starboard side.

The Herald 700 was projected to carry 52 passengers at 30in pitch plus baggage over a stage length of 1,070 nautical miles with full reserves – a 20 per cent improvement in range compared with the Series 200. A high-density version was drawn up to seat 60 passengers. None were built.

Series 800: This had the same relationship to the Series 700 as the Series 400 did to the 200, being the military version of the model. None built.

HPR4: Production HPR3 Heralds, seating a maximum of 44 passengers, were to be designated HPR4. No more machines with the Leonides engine were built, and the two prorotypes of the HPR3 were converted to the HPR7 Dart Herald.

HPR5: This was the Marathon 2 powered by two Leonides. The aircraft flew with this designation from March 1955 to 1958. Only one was converted, the engines being installed in replicas of the nacelles for the HPR3. Used by Alvis as a test bed.

HPR8: This was a projected car-carrying and freighter development of the basic jet-prop Herald airframe to meet a detailed specialist requirement put forward by Silver City Airways. The aircraft could carry nine short tons in a fuselage 15ft wide. Emphasis was on quick turn-rounds, facilitated by the low floor height of 2ft 11in. Length of the freight door was 45ft 6in.

Handley Page said the HPR8 would also be ideal as a short-range 100-passenger transport with retractable undercarriage, for transporting mining or oil drilling equipment, famine or flood relief, police or army operations, and for transporting cattle or even pilgrims! In its air ferry form, it was designed for operation between Lydd and Le Touquet with a typical load of six cars and 25 passengers or four large cars and 25 passengers. Many Herald tools and jigs were to be used, giving an enormous saving in time and cost. Engines chosen were two Rolls-Royce Dart R Da 10s. None built.

HP124: This was the projected rear-loading door version of the military Herald, powered by Rolls-Royce Dart 542-10 engines of 2,775 s.h.p. and designed for air dropping. AUW was 48,000lb.

It was entered for the RAF design competition in 1961 as a Valetta replacement for Transport Command. The Air Staff said 45 tactical transports were needed, and preferred the HP124 to its more expensive competitor, the Avro-designed HS780. The Minister of Aviation, Mr Peter Thorneycroft, would not place a contract for the HP124, unless it was with either the British Aircraft Corporation or Hawker Siddeley. Sir Frederick would not merge with either company unless a proper take-over bid was offered. HS would not bid higher than 15 shillings per share, while Sir Frederick valued his company at 42 shillings. Most expert opinion agrees that the RAF lost out on an excellent transport suited to its immediate needs. The Avro entry gained the contract and entered service with the RAF as the Andover C1 (Avro 748 MF Andover). None built.

HP125: In 1961 the company tendered a design, an extension of the HP124, to NATO Basic Military Requirement No 4. It incorporated underwing pods containing 18 vertical lift Rolls-Royce RB162 turbojets. But for the pods, the design was very similar to the HP124. None built.

HP127 'Jet Herald': A modified version of the Herald with a longer fuselage for 70 passengers. The shorter span wing had two Rolls-Royce Spey turbo-fan engines in underwing pods. Cruise speed 455 m.p.h. Employed much existing Herald structure.

Handley Page said in 1962 that future town-to-town services would demand the speed and comfort of longer-range aircraft equipped with turbo-fan engines. Because of the proved excellence of the basic Herald design, it could be adapted more quickly and far more cheaply than any other aircraft competing for this large market.

The HP127 could have been in service by 1965. The turbo-fan engines would have produced a nominal static thrust of 8,850lb at sea level. Two-abreast seating each side of a wide aisle, and pressurisation at 6 p.s.i., giving the cabin sea level pressure at altitudes up to 15,000ft. Above this, and up to Jet Herald's 27,000ft ceiling for longer-range cruising (44 passengers up to 1,280 miles), cabin pressure was to be maintained at the equivalent of 8,000ft.

The Jet Herald was not intended to replace the Dart Herald, but to complement it. Take-off weight 53,000lb, landing weight 50,000lb, ZFW 44,000lb. None built.

HP129 'Mini Herald': This was an alternative to the HP127, using the same Spey turbofans to carry 30 passengers faster in a smaller cabin. Wing span was 57ft 4in. Neither design attracted much interest, although offered at a very competitive £500,000 or less. None built.

HP131: A variation of HP124, the HP131 was entered for Belgian military design competition. Utilising 80 per cent of the Herald jigs and tools, its maximum take-off weight was set at 48,000lb. Powered by 3,245 s.h.p. Dart R Da 12 engines. Basic operating weight 27,629lb. Maximum payload 14,300lb. None built.

HP132: This project had two auxiliary General Electric CF700 B2 turbo-fan engines, each of 4,200lb thrust, mounted in wing-tip pods. Otherwise it was the same as the HP131. Its jet engines could be used for both take-off assistance and high-speed cruise. AUW increased to 50,000lb. Maximum cruising speed 325kt. None built.

HP133: Two Rolls-Royce RB162-34 engines installed in the basic HP131 design. Jet engines housed in extensions of main engine nacelles, derated to 4,200lb thrust to ensure safe running conditions with the intake in the propeller slipstream. Maximum take-off weight 48,000lb. None built.

Malaysian Ferry Flight

A trip to Malaysia was rewarded by a flight back on a Herald bought from the Royal Malaysian Air Force by British Air Ferries. It turned out to be the proverbial trip of a lifetime. While I was researching the sturdy little Herald, British Air Ferries decided to buy all eight of those no longer needed by the RMAF to add to their growing fleet.

The short-haul Herald can only fly for four hours or so at a stretch, so in all we had to make 13 refuelling and night stops on the 8,000-mile journey back home – taking in such exotic destinations as Bangkok, Rangoon, India, Pakistan and the Middle East before returning to the cold and gloom of an English winter – and the start of firemen's strike.

My instructions were to make my own way out to Kuala Lumpur and the delightful Hotel Merlin, and wait for the crew to arrive later in the week.

Once in Malaysia, it would take (theoretically) three days for our visas to enter Burma to come through. In the event, it took over a week, which meant many extra hours sunning ourselves by the crystal-clear blue waters of the hotel's swimming pool.

To be truthful I wasn't looking forward to the 17hr, one-stop flight out to Malaysia. Such long hauls can become boring and exhausting, and downright uncomfortable. I flew courtesy of the national carrier, Malaysian Airline System (MAS), on one of their last Boeing 707 flights before DC-10s took over on the London-KL route.

Right from the start, despite being delayed two hours at Heathrow because of the antics of the assistant air traffic controllers over their pay dispute, I felt this flight was going to be something special, and I wasn't disappointed.

Malaysians have an inbred tradition of gracious hospitality, engendered in their own homes, where everyone is treated like somebody very special.

You couldn't ask for more, but if you did, you jolly well got it! Free champagne or liqueurs, or an excellent dinner, continental breakfast and lunch, and free postcards plus stamps to the folks missing out back home. Other nice touches were sweets before take-off and steaming hot towels to wash your hands and face. And none of those plastic knives and forks – they were all silver.

Malaysia certainly is a seducer *par excellence.* Hot, humid, lush and modern, the country has all the colour and glamour of the orient.

It is indeed difficult not to fall in love with its peoples and respect and enjoy their customs, festivals and traditions.

Soon the day arrived when we had to start ferrying Herald *Yankee Echo* back to its homeland. But first it had to be flown from the military airfield at Sungei Besi to Subang International Airport, a few miles away. Sungei Besi is blessed with large tin deposits, which affect the accuracy of an aeroplane's compass. Some of the Heralds had been standing on the baking tarmac for nearly two years. During checks on one aircraft, an engineer opened a wing panel to have a five-foot python fall on him. Less of a problem were birds which had built their nests in the tails and control surfaces.

During the monsoon season, which had just begun, local airmen ran for cover whenever the heavy rains and lightning started. British engineers wondered why, until they realised that the tin deposits nearby were a magnet for the lightning.

Trouble getting visas to enable us to refuel in Burma delayed out departure for days. The Burmese embassy in KL would not give us the all-clear – we had to wait for confirmation in writing from Rangoon.

We checked out of the hotel twice, thinking we were on our way, only to return for a third time. Eventually we did get away for our first stop – Bangkok. We had loads of drinks on board, especially welcome in 'dry' cities like Karachi and Calcutta.

You never walk alone on the streets of Bangkok after 1 a.m. – a lesson learnt the hard way. I decided a post-midnight ramble after a good meal and show was a good idea. I had only ventured a few hundred yards from my hotel when a police car drew up and two men inside called me over. In their little English, I gathered I had broken the curfew.

My apologies and ignorance of the fact did little to alter their decision that I must get into the car and accompany them to the police station. After about half an hour of filling in and signing forms, when I thought at best my chances would be a night in the cells, I was taken from office to office and eventually told to pay about 200 Bahts (about £6).

More form-filling followed, then, with my knees trembling and with profuse apologies, I was driven back to my hotel – a free man again!

Next morning we were off to Rangoon, where, before landing, were 'buzzed' by a Thai jet fighter. At the airport workers asked us for any ballpoints, soft drinks or books or magazines.

At Calcutta we had an armed guard looking after our aeroplane. Another rifle-carrying sentry was detached to stand by the Herald as we unloaded, watched by a pair of curious and tame Indian crows. Not surprisingly, we enjoyed lovely cups of tea at the nearby hotel. The plush establishment near the airport was a complete contrast to the surrounding area, with its shanties and animals roaming all over the roads.

Our licensed engineer, John Daubney, was still suffering badly from a stomach bug picked up days before in Malaysia. At one stage he was so ill he thought he wouldn't see his wife and kids again.

Next stop was Delhi, and then Karachi, a sector which became pretty chilly. The warm air from the cabin air blowers was very welcome.

Karachi is one of those places where you wonder how cars miss each other. Our taxi to town, ten miles away, was falling to bits, and the driver had a disconcerting habit of turning round and talking for long periods of time, his eyes everywhere except on the road ahead.

I never saw Capt John Woodhouse without a lighted cigarette the whole trip.

'Look after your own bags, always take my advice, don't be a nuisance and always know where everybody else is', were the BAF's operation director's words of wisdom.

The other crew man was First Officer Derrick Parr, jokingly known as 'FO Parr', and easily recognisable by his RAF-type handlebar moustache.

On to 30°C plus at Dubai. Quick and efficient refuelling soon saw us winging our way to Baghdad, where Derrick was feeling decidedly below par, for we had just completed two 14hr days of hard flying.

Landing in windy Larnaca in Cyprus, we felt we were nearing home again. Our clean rooms faced the beach where we could watch a glorious sunrise. After taking on fuel and leaving Athens, we had to return - we had no clearance to Rome. This meant night-stopping in Greece and working out a new route.

Athens seemed full of police and political pamphlets, as elections were near. Posters seemed to be plastered everywhere. On leaving we flew over the Acropolis, making for Zagreb. We were nearing England - after a very bumpy approach Yugoslavia offered us low cloud, rain and a freezing wind.

We had a rough ride to Nice, and Capt Woodhouse had to contend with wind shear, cloud and sudden drops in speed. He did a marvellous job, as the autopilot failed early on. Nice was supposed to be our last stop before Southend, but strong headwinds over France forced us to land at Le Touquet to take on more fuel. Here we experienced a very nasty crosswind on landing. Luckily we had the skill of Capt Woodhouse up front.

Shortly afterwards, we were back on home ground. Farewells were said, customs seen to, and baggage collected. It was an experience I will never forget. As John Daubney happily observed, although we had been together constantly for over two weeks, we had never got on each others' nerves or had a row.

VIP Herald

Heads of State; military and industrial leaders; top executives in a hurry; these were the people for whom Handley Page designed their VIP or five-star Herald. A personal or corporate aircraft must be able to operate from small airfields and outback areas in addition to well-equipped airports. Using a Herald, executives could easily visit remote sites, such as oil fields and mines, where a major airport might be far away. A VIP aircraft must also be economical, fast and relatively quiet. Handley Page claimed that its Herald was one of the most economical aeroplanes in its class, and its low purchase price, low insurance rates and the support of world-wide servicing organisation should have appealed to cost-conscious owners.

The other basic requirements of a corporate aircraft are comfort and ample space to move around in. These the Herald certainly had, with its 339 sq ft of cabin floor space and an exceptionally large baggage compartment.

However, although many top people flew in Heralds, the type never flew in VIP guise. One early VIP who often took the controls of any Herald in which he happened to be flying in was King Hussein of Jordan. Accompanied by the late Aristotle Onassis, the Greek shipowner, their Serene Highnesses Prince Rainier and Princess Grace of Monaco flew from Nice to London in a Dart Herald. So, too, did Dr Arturo Frondizi, the president of the Argentine, when he flew from Holland across the North Sea for his state visit to England in 1960.

Many statesmen from Africa inspected and flew in Heralds, and Ghana's High Commissioner Mr E. O. Asau-Adjaji once piloted the aeroplane. With Mr W. Nash, then New Zealand's Prime Minister as passenger, it was a Herald that had the distinction of being the first aircraft to take-off in very bad weather conditions from Wellington's new airport after it had been officially opened in 1959.

The seal of approval on the Herald's use as a VIP transport came when Prince Philip chose it for his South American tour in 1962 (q.v.). Shortly afterwards, BUA took delivery of the first Herald in VIP fit, and operated it for several years. Handley Page hoped it would attract sales in the USA, but these never materialised.

In VIP configuration, first-class seating was provided by fully- or semi-reclining chairs and divans which could be converted into rest couches. Most layouts were arranged with staff quarters aft of the flight deck. The cabin layouts and interior fittings were developed by Handley Page and Charles Butler Associates, the aircraft interior designers. The spacious private cabin could also be fitted with reclining chairs, a table, fitted cabinets and a cloak compartment.

Forward of the lounge was a conference room, which could double as a dining room. Full course in-flight meals could be served. Tables were

The spacious crew quarters of G-ASBP (c/n 163) while operated by British United in executive fit. (Handley Page)

detachable and cabinets were designed to house ground-to-air telephones, radio, Dictaphones and similar equipment.

Single or double main entrance doors could be fitted, the large doors being especially useful for loading bulky display equipment in a flying showroom. Provision was also made for built-in power-operated passenger steps to eliminate the need for a ground crew and airfield equipment.

BUA's VIP Herald was used by the airline's senior executives and could carry long-range tanks under the wings. To ensure that the Herald (G-ASBP) did not spend too much time on the ground, BUA made the aircraft available to other companies when not needed. G-APWA was leased to BUA at Gatwick in 1962 in executive configuration.

BAF VIP HERALD

BAF's VIP executive interior for their Heralds has met with great success. When flying in the VIP role, a Herald is fitted out with only 23 seats, compared with the usual 50. There are three air hostesses, and the aeroplane is fully equipped with audio and video systems to help in sales presentations. There is plenty of room in the walk-around interior for conferences both in the air and on the ground.

Mike Keegan, chairman of BAF, says his Heralds will enable businessmen to have their conferences at airports, avoiding the need to hire expensive hotel suites. The Heralds are also cheaper to hire than the equivalent first-class fare per person on other biz jets such as the HS125, and on stage lengths up to 350 miles they are as fast as smaller machines. The VIP trips are flown by BAF's flight crews. The interior can be changed from scheduled passenger seats to VIP interior at short notice.

The first executive charter with G-BDFE was by United Willow Offshore Services Ltd of Humberside on February 14, 1976, the firm's logo being applied to the aircraft. United Towing Ltd took a party of guests and senior executives from Humberside to Rotterdam on February 16, 1976, for the launching of a new oilfield service tug named *Guardsman.*

BAF report enthusiastic support for their VIP Heralds, with charters well booked. They claim their VIP Herald offers a greater degree of comfort, service and flexibility both in flight and on the ground than any other executive aircraft available for charter in Europe. It is definitely one of the few aircraft for charter in Europe in which one can comfortably get up and walk about. The aircraft is available for charter to any European destination. The south of France is about 3hr flying time from Southend, Frankfurt 2½hr and Oslo about 4hr. The Company encourages those who charter their Heralds to treat them as their own.

Accidents

The Herald story has never been a happy one. The hoped-for orders (remember, Handley Page estimated there was a market for 400 Heralds in Latin America alone!) never materialised, and by the late 'sixties only the odd one or two were coming off the production before it closed down. Shortly after that came the collapse of Handley Page.

The tragic loss of the first Dart prototype in 1958 dealt a bitter blow to the company, and probably affected the decision of many operators toying with the idea of placing firm orders, but even if it had not crashed, the Dart-powered Herald came too late for the market. A sorry tale indeed for such a fine and robust aeroplane.

Nearly a fifth of all Heralds built have been written off in accidents, but statistics can be misleading. If only two aircraft of a particular type are built and one crashes, it could be argued that 50 per cent of the type have met with disaster. It sounds a frighteningly high proportion. Only 50 Heralds were eventually built; even so, to lose ten or more in a little over 20 years is not very good. However it should be borne in mind the Herald was built for short- and medium-range services. The average sector time of Air UK, one of the biggest Herald operators, is only about half an hour, and it is not uncommon for Heralds to be kept flying for 12 or more hours in every 24. The rate of take-offs and landings per flying hour is thus far higher than for many larger aircraft. Some of Air UK's Heralds have flown well over 20,000hr and made 30,000 landings, yet despite this high utilisation the airline has experienced remarkably little trouble with the type.

One of the earliest Herald accidents involved G-APWG of Jersey Airlines. In May 1962, a day after delivery, *Whisky Golf* was crew training near Jersey when it had to be flown back to Radlett with the starboard main undercarriage locked in the 'up' position. The Herald suffered minor damage following a belly landing. An undercarriage door jack had been incorrectly assembled.

Another early incident involved Alia Herald JY-ACR, which landed with its nosewheel up at Beirut on February 19, 1964. The nose leg would not lower, although the main undercarriage operated normally. No one was injured, and the aircraft only suffered slight damage.

Major problems arose in early 1965. On March 17 Eastern Provincial Herald CF-NAF came down near Upper Musquodoboit in Nova Scotia, killing the five passengers and three crew on board. It was the first fatal accident involving the Herald. Less than a month later, another Alia Herald, JY-ACQ, met its fate when it crashed at Demas, killing 45 – the highest number of people to die in any Herald disaster.

After these two major accidents all Herald operators were warned to look for suspected under-floor skin and stringer corrosion by 'bilge fluid' – a dangerous mixture of urine, nicotine and bar spillage – and to reduce cabin pressure till further notice. The original differential of 3.35 p.s.i. had been upped in 1964 to 4.2 p.s.i. In the middle of April 1965 the ARB and Handley Page issued an agreed 'alert bulletin' giving recommended repair schemes and limiting cabin differential pressure to 3 p.s.i. on all Heralds up to six months old, to 2 p.s.i. on those between six and 12 months and to zero on all over a year old.

All aircraft over 18 months old were grounded for examination. The remaining Alia Herald and one of BEA's revealed signs of corrosion. All Heralds were recalled in turn to Radlett for their inter-chine belly structure to be renewed, reskinned and internally painted with an anti-corrosive heat-cured epoxy resin.

In mid-May 1965 it was discovered that BMA's Herald, G-ASKK, had corrosion in the chine top-hat section, causing pressure differential to be reduced from 4 to 2.5 p.s.i.

A nail-biting incident that nearly involved the loss of FM1020 of the Royal Malaysian Air Force occurred on July 21, 1966. Flt Lt (now Sqn Ldr) Norman Rose was training another pilot at the time. They were on finals, and shortly after selecting full flap, there was a bang and the aircraft rolled violently to port.

'The chap I was training didn't know what to do', said Flt Lt Rose, 'as one flap went down while the other wouldn't. I applied full aileron and starboard rudder but couldn't stop the roll.' Handley Page said asymmetric flap was impossible, but it happened sure enough.

With the wings vertical, Rose had his hands on the flying controls, and told his student to raise flaps. Control was finally regained only a few feet above the trees on approach. An overshoot was made and a safe flapless landing carried out. The cause was found to be asymmetric flap caused by a control chain breaking and fracturing the chain guard.

But for the skill, presence of mind and capability of Flt Lt Rose, this technical failure would almost certainly have ended in the loss of the aircraft and crew. As the incident happened over a heavily-populated area, the outcome could have been far worse. Rose was awarded a Green Endorsement in his log book for his flying skill.

A day later another RMAF Herald took off from Tawau for Labuan. At 10,500ft the crew was told that 'all Heralds have been grounded', and for the next half-hour the two pilots sat in the cockpit, wondering what, if anything, was going to happen.

The incident was, in fact, the outcome of the malfunction of the flap on FM1020. The technical staff worked hard inspecting and rectifying this serious defect and all aircraft were flying again within two weeks.

The next fatal accident involving a Herald came when PP-SDJ of Sadia crashed on Marumbi Peak near Curitiba, in Brazil, on November 3, 1967. The cause of the crash, which claimed the lives of all five crew members and 16 passengers, was attributed to pilot error. Four passengers escaped.

Another very serious incident happened on February 24, 1969. Far Eastern Air Transport Herald B-2009 was lost with the lives of 36 people when it made a forced landing and struck a ditch near Tainan, and an engine caught fire.

RMAF Herald FM1024 made a wheels-up landing at Changi on April 18, 1968, but was flying again a week later. Another RMAF Herald, FM1025, also suffered a wheels-up landing on January 17, 1976, and was reported to be beyond economical repair (the Air Force was shortly to phase out the type and replace it with Hercules transports).

Air Manila's PI-C869 had no luck. It was damaged at Davao on August 13, 1967. It was subsequently repaired, but then had the great misfortune to be written off in November 1970 when a hangar collapsed on it during a typhoon.

One of Itavia's Heralds, I-TIVE, was written off on a crew training flight at Rome's Ciampino airport. In April 1971 a survey was carried out into its possible repair, but it was subsequently broken up. Some parts went to BIA.

The three ex-BEA and Autair Heralds that went to Urraca of Columbia in 1970 have fared badly. All have been involved in accidents, two having been written off. At the time of writing, the remaining one (HK-715) is reported to be flying still. HK-721 was destroyed at Valledupar on May 7, 1972, and it was reported that HK-718 was severely damaged in a wheels-up landing on August 3, 1973. This Herald must have been repaired, because on November 2 that year it made another emergency landing with undercarriage trouble at Villavicencio. There were 12 people on board, of whom six were killed and the others injured. This time HK-718 was written off.

HK-715 made a belly landing at Villavicencio on March 17, 1974. The accident was due to the failure of the outer port wheel, the tyre of which burst on take-off from Cacuta. A piece of rubber hit the electrical system of the port landing gear doors valve, and the doors failed to operate when the aircraft landed at Arauca, so the pilot diverted to Villavicencio and made a perfect belly landing. The fuselage and VHF antenna were damaged, the port landing gear was destroyed and both propellers were twisted. Both engines were shock loaded. The same aircraft was involved in another accident at Hato la Libertad on June 23, 1975.

In recent years Heralds of Arkia, BIA, and BAF have been involved in minor to fairly major incidents, many involving the undercarriage. The Herald does have the odd problem with bursting tyres, although landing in a crosswind obviously has its problems.

On September 4, 1973, as the engines of BIA Herald G-APWF were shut down in the parking area at Gatwick, the crew noticed that the nose was slowly sinking. Investigations revealed that the front pressure bulkhead around the nose gear downlock had failed and allowed the downlock catch to disengage. Although the four crew and 41 passengers were uninjured, reports said there was 'substantial' damage to *Whisky Foxtrot*.

Sister ship G-APWE, also owned by BIA, was reported to have run off the runway while landing in a crosswind at Guernsey early in 1974. The accident closed the airport save for a restricted landing area, although the aircraft was apparently undamaged.

A more worrying incident happened on Christmas Eve, 1974. Yet another

BIA machine was involved, this time G-BBXJ, piloted by C. Henshaw. The Herald had to make an emergency landing at Jersey and was badly damaged. Bound from Southampton to Guernsey, G-BBXJ took off late at 6.25 p.m. because of engine problems. On the cross-Channel journey the starboard engine was feathered and the crew decided to divert to Jersey. With one engine out, the aircraft landed heavily, causing the undercarriage to fail. It veered off the runway and travelled backwards across the grass for some 200ft, coming to rest astride a fence in front of a small wood.

Eye witnesses said the aeroplane suffered a damaged starboard wing and badly damaged floor, undercarriage and propellers. There was no fire, and none of the 53 people on board was hurt. All flew on to Guernsey about an hour later. G-BBXJ was written off. The remains of the wings could be seen in the BIA hangar at Southampton while the fuselage was used for fire practice at the 09 runway end at Jersey.

G-APWF had an undercarriage collapse during take-off on runway 26 at Gatwick on July 20, 1975, while on a flight to Guernsey. The aircraft was badly damaged but none of the 49 passengers was injured.

BIA were plagued with yet more undercarriage problems with G-ASBG. Just two months later, on September 14, two wheels on the aircraft burst. Smoke was reported to be coming from the port wheels and two loud bangs were heard when the plane landed at Exeter with 52 passengers and crew. Damage was confined to the undercarriage, wheels and tyres.

Arkia still flew four Heralds until recently. 4X-AHN, the last Herald built, was reported damaged when it fell off jacks at David Ben Gurion airport during maintenance on June 25, 1974. The same aircraft struck a ground power unit at Dov Hoss airport, Tel Aviv, on December 9, 1974.

Another Arkia machine, 4X-AHS, was extensively damaged in a wheels-up landing at Ben Gurion airport on August 28, 1975. There were no casualties.

4X-AHT suffered a starboard undercarriage collapse while taxiing at Lod airport, Tel Aviv, on December 18, 1972. The fuselage and starboard wing and engine were damaged. The same aircraft also suffered a hangar accident on December 15, 1975. During nose undercarriage servicing the port main undercarriage ground lock became detached, and the aircraft fell to the ground, resulting in damage to the port aileron, propeller blade and under-fuselage skinning.

BMA's G-BAVX was said to have been damaged at Aberdeen in early September 1974, and G-BCZG of BAF had a nose wheel collapse at Southend after landing from Ostend on July 1, 1975.

Airlines that didn't take delivery

Several airlines paid an unusual compliment to a private venture civil aircraft when they ordered the Herald 'off the drawing board' before it had made its first flight.

In the mid-'fifties Handley Page was so confident its new aircraft was going to be a big hit that they planned to lay down the necessary jigs and tools for the building of 100 piston-engined Herald branchliners. It was expected that deliveries to airlines would be started towards the end of 1957. As we have already seen, this was not to be.

The confident decision to go ahead and construct 100 Heralds (in four batches of 25) followed orders from three airlines for this maid-of-all-work aircraft. By the time G-AODE made its maiden flight in August 1955, Handley Page had received firm orders for 29 Heralds. Price was then around £145,000, as opposed to about £27,000 for a Dakota in good condition.

QUEENSLAND AIRLINES

This Australian airline became the first operator to order the Herald, doing so late in 1954. It intended to use the type on its network of routes on the eastern coast of the continent. G-AODE was originally rolled out in the colours of Queensland Airlines, with a dark blue cheat line on the fuselage and the QAL insignia on the nose and Queensland titling on the fuselage.

The Herald's first public appearance was at the 1955 Farnborough air show, when it still wore Queensland Airlines livery. The aircraft's front door was designed around the shape of a wool bale, as requested by the Australians. Unfortunately, when the time was approaching to put pen to paper, the airline fought shy of a new aeroplane and its associated teething troubles.

AUSTRALIAN NATIONAL AIRWAYS

Australian National Airways, in the mid-'fifties the largest privately-owned airline in Australia, also chose the Herald to replace its DC-3s on its medium-range services. Capt I. N. Holyman, ANA's managing director, said in 1955 that few aircraft constructors showed a real appreciation of the need for a composite passenger and freight carrying aircraft, but that Handley Page was an exception. The two Australian options were cancelled by Ansett's purchase of ANA and rationalisation of their equipment with Butlers, who controlled Queensland Airlines.

• • •

Heralds for both Australian airlines were to enter service with rearward facing seats. This feature, which had been the practise for years on Handley Page

Hastings with RAF Transport Command, became an official requirement for new civil aircraft imported into Australia after January 1, 1957.

LLOYD AEREO COLOMBIANO

This South American airline was the third in the Herald queue to order the type before it had flown. It began operating in 1954 with Curtiss C-46s and a DC-3 on local routes in Colombia and a service to Miami. The contract was dogged by currency problems.

• • •

The second Herald prototype, which flew a year after the first in August 1956, was to be used for development flying and, later, to go on overseas tours to show airlines exactly how the Herald would operate on their routes.

The Herald was one of the few entirely new aircraft at the 1955 Farnborough air display, and attracted a lot of attention, having made its maiden flight only a week before. In three days of concentrated test flying it put in more than ten airborne hours to prove itself before being displayed in the air at Farnborough. Few prototypes can have been flown so intensively straight after their first flight.

Representatives of many airlines and air forces inspected the Herald at the air show or later at Reading. They included visitors from airlines in Britain, Eire, Africa, Australia, Cyprus, Malaya, New Zealand, Belgium, the Sudan, Switzerland, South America and the United States. Interest from the USA was shown by Piedmont Airlines, Bonanza Airlines and Wien Alaska Airlines.

• • •

AIR KRUISE (KENT) LTD

Soon after the 1955 Farnborough show the first British order was announced by Air Kruise, an associate company of Silver City Airways. The airline planned to buy at least six Heralds for further development of coach-air-rail travel between London, Paris and Brussels.

Announcing the order, Mr Eoin C. Mekie, chairman of British Aviation Services - of which Air Kruise was a subsidiary company, together with Silver City Airways, Aquila Airways and Britavia - said the Herald would supplement and eventually replace the Dakotas and Bristol Freighters used on the airline's passenger services across the English Channel and on its continental air-coach tours. It was ideally suited to the short- and medium-range traffic of Air Kruise. It could use smaller airfields but still had the speed, range and pressurised cabin to take passengers to distant European resorts. However, Air Kruise (Kent) was taken over by British Aviation Services, and the provisional order was dropped.

• • •

A 19-day world tour that Handley Page deputy chairman Air Cdre A. V. Harvey went on during 1955 evoked further overseas interest in this sturdy transport. Negotiations started with a Malayan airline for six Heralds, with a possible option on four more. Air Cdre Harvey combined business and fact-finding on his tour, which took in India, Singapore, Australia, Fiji, Hawaii and America. Several airlines in these countries hinted that they might become Herald users in the future.

In December that year the company's sales manager, Grp Capt Collard, spent three weeks in the Middle East and visited Turkey, the Lebanon, Syria, Iraq, Jordan, Egypt and Kuwait, where he met potential buyers, and in 1956 Handley Page representatives visited Afghanistan, Iran, Italy, Germany, Iceland and Australia. In most countries more than one airline was visited.

Enthusiasm about the Herald was not limited to requests for visits by the company's personnel. Airline operators from many countries came to Radlett and Woodley aerodromes to study the machine for themselves. In that year representatives of no fewer than 33 airlines visited Handley Page, and most of them flew in the Herald. They came from places as far afield as central Africa, Australia, the Philippines, New Zealand, India, Burma, Japan, the United States, Colombia, Hawaii and Afghanistan. Route analyses were prepared for 43 airlines by request.

Several other operators were to order the new-style Herald with Rolls-Royce Darts, but for various reasons failed to take delivery.

NORTH-SOUTH AIRLINES

This small British independent was formed in 1959 and operated seasonal services from Leeds/Bradford to Exeter, Bournemouth and the Isle of Wight. It planned to concentrate on charter work when it placed an order for one Herald Series 100 for delivery in 1961. This order was not confirmed.

CAMBRIAN AIRWAYS

Cambrian Airways, which began scheduled services in 1949 and concentrated on serving South Wales and the West of England, was considering ordering up to four Heralds in 1962, presumably to replace its large fleet of DC-3s. One was on order in 1962, but was never delivered.

CRUZ AIRWAYS

Cruz Airways was formed in 1962 to try and convince the Philippine Civil Aeronautics Board there was a case for competition on domestic routes. The airline's president, J. P. Cruz, signed a contract for two Heralds in Manila in December 1962, but the airline ceased operation and went bankrupt in the summer of 1963 before taking delivery. At the time the first aircraft was already painted and registered PI-C910 (CF-MCK, one of the two orginally completed for MCA). After the Cruz order was cancelled, this aircraft went to Sadia and then to BMA. It is now operated by Air UK.

During the latter part of 1963 Autair operated PI-C910 (re-registered

G-ASKK) in Cruz Airways colours. Colour scheme was chocolate and gold with Autair titling on the fuselage and with a white fuselage top, and colourful tropical fish insignia on a white shield on either side of the forward fuselage between the cockpit and cabin windows.

AIR COMORES

Formed in 1963, Air Comores operates scheduled passenger and cargo services within the Comoro Islands in the Indian Ocean, linking Moroni with Anjouan, Dzaoudzi, Moheli, Dar-es-Salaam and Mombasa. In 1974 it was reported that TransBrasil was negotiating to sell possibly two of its Herald fleet to the airline, but it never did. Another source indicated that the two FAT Heralds were to be sold to Air Comores.

VASP (VIACAO AEREA SAO PAULO)

This large Brazilian domestic operator ordered ten of the Series 700 in April 1965 for delivery starting in 1966. VASP was the first to place an order for the projected 52-seater; it was worth £3¾ million with spares. The airline took inspiration from the way Sadia operated its Heralds and would probably have eventually bought even more Heralds to replace its 25-30 older DC-3s and C-46s. About this time Handley Page indicated that the Herald could be assembled and even manufactured in Brazil, in view of the potential size of the market in South America.

G-AODF (c/n 148) in early-style BEA livery circa 1959. Note narrow "BEA" letters and registration at top of fin.

G-ARTC (c/n 148) Herald Series 200 in Maritime Central livery. (Handley Page)

Early days for Heralds in airline service . . . G-APWB (c/n 150) on lease to Jersey Airlines at Gatwick July 1962.

Out of service. G-APWB (c/n 150) at Luton after flying with BEA and sold to Autair. (Philip Birtles)

G-APWC (c/n 151) in flight showing off her large flaps. (APN)

G-APWC (c/n 151) in Autair colours.

G-APWE (c/n 153) in BIA livery at Prestwick March 16, 1972. Whisky Echo has flown with Air UK and its predecessors since 1961. (Philip Birtles)

G-APWF (c/n 154) at Newcastle May 4, 1963. Note Jersey Airlines livery, but "British United" titling under windows. (Ian MacFarlane)

Various trial paint schemes were tried out before BIA settled on its final livery. Here G-APWF (c/n 154) comes in to land at Gatwick with a white tail fin bearing the words "British Island" in black. (APN)

Another experimental colour scheme. This time G-APWF (c/n 154) sports stripes on the fin. Pictured at Woolsington September 11, 1977. (MAP/Ian MacFarlane)

A fine low-level shot of G-APWG (c/n 155) in its new British United colours at the Farnborough air show in 1968.

The ill-fated G-APWI (c/n 157) at Newcastle June 3, 1963 in British United colours. This Herald was written off in Taiwan in 1969. (Ian MacFarlane)

Another Herald livery rarely seen. Autair briefly operated G-ASKK (c/n 161) in the Cruz Airways colours of chocolate and gold with Autair titles in dark blue. Seen at Edinburgh in September 1963.
(Peter R. Keating)

Far Eastern Air Transport Herald B-2001 (c/n 162) wears its British registration G-ATHB prior to delivery in February 1966. This aircraft is now derelict at Taipei. (Handley Page)

Munich in early May 1968 saw G-AVPN (c/n 176) in service in full Itavia colours. It later became I-TIVB with the Italian operator. (MAP)

G-BAVX (c/n 194) shows signs of former Brazilian ownership at East Midlands Airport. (APN)

G-BCZG (c/n 159) *Rupert Keegan* starts up at Southend in front of G-BCWE. Both wear the original BAF Herald livery. (BAF)

G-BDFE (c/n 167) again, with "VIP Dart Herald" painted on the engine nacelle. Amsterdam February 1978. (Rob Hemelrijk)

G-BDZV (c/n 191) on July 23, 1976 sporting the new livery. Note the absence of any name. (BAF)

Back from the Far East. G-BEYK (c/n 187) engineless at Southend before moving into the hangar for overhaul. Note "27" on nosewheel door (formerly FM-1027). (Peter J. Bish)

G-BFRJ (c/n 195) wears Express Air Service titles, previously Express Air Freight. Pictured at Woolsington November 1, 1978. (MAP/Ian MacFarlane)

Herald CF-NAC (c/n 159) at Prestwick February 17, 1962 on delivery flight to Nordair of Canada. Note long-range fuel tank under wing. (R.A. Watt)

CF-MCK (c/n 161) at Farnborough September 6, 1962 in Maritime Central colours. It was never delivered. (Peter R. Keating)

CF-EPC (c/n 167) in original Eastern Provincial colour scheme, with large EPA letters on fin, on its delivery flight to Canada. Photographed at Prestwick March 30, 1963. (R.A. Watt)

D-BEBE (c/n 179) *Herald of Bavaria*. It now flies with Air UK as G-AYMG. (APN)

Europe Aero Service Herald F-BOIZ (c/n 188). (MAP)

RMAF Herald FM-1025 (c/n 181). Although allocated the registration G-BEYI, this Herald suffered an accident in Malaysia and never returned to its homeland. (MAP)

The sun shines fitfully down on FM-1027 (c/n 187) at Kuala Lumpur. (MAP)

Globe Air Herald HB-AAK (c/n 162) *Herald of Bern* at Hatfield. (Philip Birtles)

An Urraca Herald Series 100 resplendent in its new paint job before delivery to Colombia.

HK-715 (c/n 151) ex-GAPWC at Prestwick October 30, 1970. (J. Guthrie)

I-TIVA (c/n 164) of Itavia with the inscription "Servizio Postale"on fin strake. (R. Riding)

Itavia Heralds adopted subtle changes in livery over the years. Here I-TIVB (c/n 176) has lost its Italian flag on the cheat line and no longer carriers the word "Aerolinee" under the passenger windows. (MAP)

I-TIVU (c/n 184) sports a far more readable identification at Milan in December 1971. The airline name also appears under the starboard wing.

PP-SDJ (c/n 190) of Sadia in its original colour scheme. It wore several variations during its sojourn in South America. (Handley Page)

TransBrasil Herald PP-SDM (c/n 149) – Whisky Alpha in disguise – lifts off from São Paulo September 15, 1973. Note the words "Dart Herald 100" on engine nacelle. (Philip Birtles)

Arkia, Israel's inland airline, stopped flying Heralds in the late 1970's. This is 4X-AHO (c/n 183). (APN)

The first Herald for the Royal Arab (Jordanian) Air Force (109 c/n 165) takes off from a snowy Radlett Airfield on January 31, 1963. (Handley Page)

The Rolls-Royce Dart

Turboprops and turbofans are logical developments of the pure jet engine. Rolls-Royce, and several other companies, became interested in this power source near the end of World War Two. Rolls-Royce modified a Derwent engine to drive a propeller, and called it the Trent. In September 1945 it was flight tested in a Meteor, which thereby gained the distinction of being the first turboprop-powered aircraft to fly.

The Dart was, in fact, Rolls-Royce's third turboprop, having succeeded the Trent and being contemporary with the higher-powered Clyde. It was originally designed as a 1,000 s.h.p. engine for two potential RAF trainers, the Avro Athena and Boulton Paul Balliol, and for commercial aircraft. A Dart-powered Athena flew in 1949, but was only used for development flying.

Design work on the engine, the RB53, had started in April 1945. Just 18 months later the first prototype engine was on test. The aim was to build a simple yet robust engine; this first experimental engine delivered only 600 s.h.p. and weighed more than 1,100lb instead of its design weight of 700lb. Eventually a weight saving of 350lb was achieved.

The prototype Dart was installed in the nose of a converted Lancaster bomber test bed, and was first flown in mid-1947. An intensive development programme then commenced at the Rolls-Royce flight test establishment at Hucknall. A converted Wellington bomber and a C-47 Dakota also joined the programme, and later a converted Ambassador. The Wellington became the first aircraft to fly powered solely by the Dart, which it did in June 1948. Based on the centrifugal compressor system, the Dart gained from a wealth of experience on superchargers for the war-time Merlin and Griffon engines.

During the war the UK aircraft industry had concentrated on producing military aircraft, and was ill-equipped to manufacture the civil transports needed in the early post-war period. Vickers-Armstrong Ltd produced a design study for a four-engined aircraft in 1945. This was the VC2 - later to develop into the immortal Viscount, the V630 prototype of which first flew in July 1948. By then the Dart had achieved 1,000 s.h.p. and its 150hr type test at the R Da 1 rating. It was installed in the Viscount, and so the lengthy process of proving and developing the power plant - and gaining general acceptance - began.

In August 1950 BEA put the 32-seat 630 into service between London, Paris and Edinburgh - the first operational services in the world by a gas turbine-powered airliner.

Two Dakotas were fitted with Darts and used by BEA as freighters on European routes from August 1951 until May 1953. Many air traffic controllers were puzzled when the C-47s reported flight levels of 25,000ft, but not a single failure occurred during this period - a sure pointer to the success story of the Dart in the years ahead.

In January 1949 a 150hr development test was run at the R Da 4 rating of 1,250 s.h.p., and in May, a further 150hr test was completed at the R Da 3 rating of 1,400 s.h.p. With this extra power a larger and faster Viscount – the 47-seat Series 700 – was built. It first flew in August 1950, and in April 1953 this aircraft began full-scale operation with BEA, the Dart thus becoming the first turboprop in the world to enter scheduled airline service. At this stage the engine was giving an initial overhaul life of 400hr. TBO (time between overhauls) was progressively raised to 1,050hr and then to 1,400hr after three years in service.

Once the Viscount was successfully in service with operators all over the globe, the development of the Dart progressed rapidly. In 1954 production began of the R Da 6, producing 1,600 s.h.p. for take-off. This entered airline service in the Viscount 800 in April that year, and proved to be one of the most reliable and economical units ever produced.

Power development beyond 1,600 s.h.p. demanded more radical modifications. Thus in 1956 a further increase in power to 1,910 s.h.p. was introduced in the fully-rated version of the R Da 7 – the engine chosen for the Handley Page Herald. This was achieved by making further changes in the reduction gear, increasing the engine mass flow and adding an extra turbine stage, making three in all. A 90 per cent increase in power was thus made, using the same basic design.

The R Da 7 first entered airline service in the Viscount 810 in April 1958. As with the R Da 3, it started operations with a TBO of 400hr, but the figure rose even more quickly than on the earlier R Da 3 and 6 engines. By November 1962 it achieved a remarkable TBO of 3,500hr.

The possibility of changing to a twin-engine formula had been under constant review during the Herald's design. Variants were projected with engines such as the Tyne and the Eland, but the Dart proved the most attractive. By 1956, as we have seen, it had only reached a 1,000hr overhaul mark in R Da 6 form – insufficient power for the Herald. At that time Handley Page was given to understand by Rolls-Royce that it was the most powerful form of Dart likely to be built!

In December 1956 a team from Handley Page visited the USA for talks on the Lycoming T53 and GEC D58 turbines, and the possibility of the Herald being built in the USA with four of either of these engines. However, work started in 1957 was abandoned after Sir Frederick's trip to New Zealand and Australia, where overwhelming preference was shown for an aircraft with only two engines. The growing faith in the Dart was very apparent, and about this time Rolls-Royce announced they were going to build the R Da 7 – a decision they would never regret.

Design work began in May 1957, and the first prototype Herald was fitted with Darts and flown in March 1958. The crash of G-AODE *en route* to Farnborough was caused by a weakness in this engine that was not present in earlier models, so modifications were required.

Having built up millions of hours of flying experience in airline service, the

Dart was obviously a highly suitable engine for military duties. The utilisation rate of military aircraft is far lower than that of civil transports, allowing engine overhaul life to be traded for higher ratings, so the R Da 8 of 2,470 s.h.p. came into being. As all civil Darts use water/methanol injection for power restoration for take-off under hot weather and/or high altitude conditions, the higher rating was attained by increasing both fuel flow and the degree of water/methanol injection. This model powered the Argosy of RAF Transport Command.

As far back as 1956 the R Da 10, designed for 2,750 s.h.p. was on the drawing board. Only the lack of a suitable application delayed its type test until 1958. Flight testing in an Airspeed Ambassador began in March 1961, and the engine entered airline service four years later. It powered the Namco YS-11, the Fairchild Hiller FH227 and Grumman Gulfstream.

As with the R Da 7 and 8, there were obvious benefits in uprating the R Da 10 to a still higher power for military use. This was done in the R Da 12 of 3,000 s.h.p., which was very suitable for military STOL transports.

Since entry into service, the Dart's power output has increased from the 1,485 total equivalent horsepower (1,107kw) of the R Da 3 rating to 3,025 t.e.h.p. (2,256kw) of the R Da 10. The military version (R Da 12) develops 3,245 t.e.h.p. (2,420kw). These increases have been made with hardly any alterations in external dimensions, yet the power/weight ratio has increased by 52 per cent.

The Dart has been chosen to power more than ten types of production aircraft. It has amassed at least 100 million hours of operation in service, its assets being reliability and ease of operation and maintenance. In 1975 the Dart was achieving an annual in-flight shutdown rate (all causes) of 0.035 per 1,000hr, ie one shutdown in flight per 28,000hr.

An annual unscheduled removal rate (all causes) of 0.26 per 1,000hr, ie one unscheduled removal per 3,840hr, is certainly an incredible achievement. The Dart is currently achieving an overhaul life of 9,000hr, and major components have achieved lives above 32,000hr.

Rolls-Royce designed the Dart as a simple, robust engine which would be easy to operate and maintain (by easy access through hinged cowlings). Dart-powered aircraft like the Herald are giving world-wide service under all climatic conditions in a variety of roles, ranging from anti-submarine patrols to short-haul passenger operation and luxury executive transport. Power output has been increased by improving the efficiency of the compressor and turbine, by introducing power boosting with water/methanol, and by using new materials to withstand the resulting higher temperatures and stresses. At the same time the reduction gear has been progressively developed to cope with the higher power.

The Herald's two R Da 7 Mark 527 Darts each give 1,910 s.h.p. at take-off plus 505lb jet thrust. The total equivalent horsepower for take-off is thus $2 \times 2{,}105$. Each engine drives a fully-feathering constant-speed auto-coarsening Rotol airscrew. The four blades are 12ft in diameter.

DART DATES

1945	Design work started
	Trent Meteor first flight
1946	First test bed run
1947	Dart first flown in Lancaster
	R Da 1 passes type test
1948	Test flight of two engines in Wellington
	First flight of Viscount 630
1949	R Da 4 passes type test
	Avro Athena first flight
	Dart Dakota first flight
1950	Viscount 630 service trials
	R Da 3 type test
1951	Dart Dakota freighter in service BEA
1953	Viscount 700 in airline service (R Da 3)
1954	R Da 6 type test
1955	Fokker Friendship first flight
1956	One million engine hours in airline service
	R Da 7 type test
1957	Viscount 800 in airline service (R Da 6)
1958	First flights Herald, Fairchild Friendship
	Fokker Friendship in service
	R Da 7 Viscount 800 in service
	2,000hr overhaul life cleared
	25hr test at 3,200 b.h.p. on R Da 10
1959	Argosy first flight
	Grumman Gulfstream in service
	400 Viscounts in service
	10 million engine hours in airline service
1960	Avro 748 first flight
	100 Dart-powered operators
	R Da 8 type test
	3,000hr overhaul life cleared
	Argosy in service
1961	Herald in service
1962	HS748 in service
	First flight YS-11
	Military Argosy in service (R Da 8)
	4,000hr overhaul life cleared
1963	200 Dart operators
	25 million engine hours in service
1964	R Da 12 type test
1965	YS-11 in service
	Dart-Convair in service
	Trial run of R Da 12 at 4,000 b.h.p.

1966 300 Dart operators
Fairchild FH227 first flight
1967 40 million hours in service
1968 45 million hours in service
1969 50 million hours in service
1970 25th anniversary of design
1974 73 million hours+ in service

LEADING DATA HPR HERALD

	HPR3	**HPR7 Series 100**	**HPR7 Series 200**	**HPR7 Series 400**
Span (ft)	94.75	94.75	94.75	(Same as Series 200)
Length (ft)	70.25	71.91	75.50	
Height (ft)	22.33	24.10	24.10	
Wing area (sq ft)	886	886	886	
Max all-up weight (lb)	37,500	41,000	43,000	
Max cruising speed (m.p.h.)	224	275	275	
Ceiling (ft)	19,900	26,700	27,900	
No. reserves range with max fuel (mls)	1,640	1,730	1,635	
Max no. of passengers	44	47	56	
Engines	4×870 h.p. Alvis Leonides Major 701/1	2×2105 eshp R-R Dart 527	2×2105 eshp R-R Dart 527	
Static thrust (lb st)		502		
Initial rate of climb (ft/min)	980	2,000	1,805	

HERALD CROSS-REFERENCE INDEX

B - TAIWAN
B-2001 162
B-2009 157
B-2011 165

CF - CANADA
CF-EPA 165
CF-EPC 167
CF-EPI 166
CF-MCK 161
CF-MCM 162
CF-NAC 159
CF-NAF 160

D - GERMANY
D-BEBE 179
D-BIBI 176
D-BOBO 165

F - FRANCE
F-BLOY 173
F-BOIZ 188
F-OCLY 173
F-OCLZ 188

FM - RMAF
FM-1020 171
FM-1021 172

FM-1022	175
FM-1023	178
FM-1024	180
FM-1025	181
FM-1026	182
FM-1027	187

G - UNITED KINGDOM

G-8-1	183
G-8-2	174
G-8-3	185
G-AODE	147
G-AODF	148
G-APWA	149
G-APWB	150
G-APWC	151
G-APWD	152
G-APWE	153
G-APWF	154
G-APWG	155
G-APWH	156
G-APWI	157
G-APWJ	158
G-ARTC	148
G-ASBF	163
G-ASBG	164
G-ASBP	163
G-ASKK	161
G-ASPJ	173
G-ASVO	185
G-ATDS	189
G-ATHB	162
G-ATHE	165
G-ATIG	177
G-AVEZ	169
G-AVPN	176
G-AYMG	179
G-BAVX	194
G-BAZJ	183
G-BBXI	184
G-BBXJ	196
G-BCWE	166
G-BCZG	159
G-BDFE	167
G-BDZV	191
G-BEBB	186
G-BEYD	171
G-BEYE	172
G-BEYF	175
G-BEYG	178
G-BEYH	180
G-BEYI	181
G-BEYJ	182
G-BEYK	187
G-BEZB	174
G-BFRJ	195
G-BFRK	197

HB - SWITZERLAND

HB-AAG	162
HB-AAH	169
HB-AAI	173
HB-AAK	173
HB-AAL	188

HK - COLOMBIA

HK-715	151
HK-718	150
HK-721	152

I - ITALY

I-TIVA	164
I-TIVB	176
I-TIVE	168
I-TIVI	196
I-TIVU	184

JY - JORDAN

JY-ACQ	170
JY-ACR	165

PI (later RP) - PHILIPPINES

PI-C866	192
PI-C869	163
PI-C910	161
RP-C866	192

PP - BRAZIL

PP-ASU	161
PP-ASV	149
PP-SDG	169
PP-SDH	185
PP-SDI	177
PP-SDJ	190
PP-SDL	191
PP-SDM	149
PP-SDN	194

VP-B - BAHAMAS

VP-BCG	167

4X - ISRAEL

4X-AHN	197
4X-AHO	195
4X-AHR	183
4X-AHS	174
4X-AHT	189

Royal Jordanian Air Force

109	165
110	170

HANDLEY PAGE HERALD
Production List

Abbreviations

C/N - Construction number
F/F - First flight
S - Sold to
D - Delivered to
RR - Re-registered
L - Leased to
Ch - Chartered
WFS - Withdrawn from service
WO - Written off
Sc - Scrapped

C/N	Registration	Owner/ Operator	Series	First flight	Delivery	Remarks
147	G-AODE	Handley Page		25/8/55		1st prototype with

						Leonides engines (HPR3).
				11/3/58		Re-engined with Rolls-Royce Darts (HPR7). WO Milford, nr Godalming, 30/8/58.
148	G-AODF	Handley Page		3/8/56		2nd prototype with Leonides (HPR3).
			100	17/12/58		Re-engined with Darts (HPR7).
			200	8/4/61		
	G-ARTC					Re-registered 8/61. Shown at Farnborough in MCA colours 9/61. WFS 5/62. Broken up Radlett and sold for scrap 69/70.
149	G-APWA	Handley Page	100	30/10/59		Demonstrator. 1st production Herald.
		Jersey Airlines			17/5/61	Leased.
		BEA			20/1/62	Leased.
		BUA (executive config.)			/62	Leased.
		Autair			4/63	Leased to 8/63.
		RMAF			31/8/63	Leased.
	PP-ASV	Sadia			20/2/64	Leased to 24/10/65.
	G-APWA	BMA			14/4/66	Leased to 9/66.
	PP-SDM	Sadia			18/11/66	Sold.
		TransBrasil				Re-registered /72.
		TABA				Leased 75/76.
						Stored at Congonhas /76.
	G-APWA	BAF			11/8/76	*Mandy Keegan*.
		Air Ecosse				Leased.
		BAF				
150	G-APWB	Jersey Airlines	101	6/7/61	27/7/61	Leased.
					10/3/62	Bought by MoA for BEA.
		Autair			28/11/66	Sold.
		Court Line Aviation				Re-registered 5/12/69.
	HK-718	Urraca			20/11/70	Sold, WO Villavicencio 2/11/73.
151	G-APWC	Jersey Airlines		23/11/61		Leased /61.
					5/1/62	Bought by MoA for BEA.
		Autair			28/11/66	Sold.
		Court Line				Re-registered

		Aviation				5/12/69.
	HK-715	Urraca			26/10/70	*Bochica*, WFS. Under repair.
152	G-APWD	BEA	101	18/4/62	30/4/62	Bought by MoA for BEA.
		Autair			28/11/66	Sold.
		Court Line Aviation				Re-registered 5/12/69.
	HK-721	Urraca			30/10/70	WO Valledupar 7/5/72.
153	G-APWE	Jersey Airlines	201	13/12/61	4/1/62	
		BU(CI) Airways				Re-registered 1/8/63.
		BUIA				Re-registered 1/11/68.
		BIA				Re-registered 20/7/70.
		Air UK				1/80.
154	G-APWF	Jersey Airlines	201	29/3/62	9/4/62	
		BU(CI) Airways				Re-registered 1/8/63.
		BUIA				Re-registered 1/11/68.
		BIA				Re-registered 20/7/70.
		Air UK				1/80.
155	G-APWG	Jersey Airlines	201	27/4/62	22/5/62	
		BU(CI) Airways				Re-registered 1/8/63.
		BUIA				Re-registered 1/11/68.
		BIA				Re-registered 20/7/70.
		Air UK				1/80.
156	G-APWH	Jersey Airlines	201	25/5/62	6/6/62	
		BU(CI) Airways				Re-registered 1/8/63.
		BUIA				Re-registered 1/11/68.
		BIA				Re-registered 20/7/70.
		Air UK				1/80.
157	G-APWI	BU(CI) Airways	201	8/5/63	24/5/63	
	B-2009	FAT			6/12/68	Sold, WO Kaohsiung 24/2/69.
		Air UK				1/80.
158	G-APWJ	BU(CI) Airways	201	29/5/63	13/6/63	
		BUIA				Re-registered 1/11/68.
		BIA				Re-registered 20/7/70.
		Air UK				1/80.

159	CF-NAC	Nordair	202	15/1/62	13/2/62	
		EPA				Re-registered /62.
	G-BCZG	BAF			3/75	*Rupert Keegan*, now *Jean Batten*.
		BIA				L. 1/1/79.
160	CF-NAF	Nordair	211	2/3/62	13/3/62	
		MCA				Re-registered /62.
		EPA				Re-registered 5/63, WO nr Upper Musquodoboit, Nova Scotia 17/3/65.
161	CF-MCK		211	5/7/62		Built for MCA. At Farnborough 9/62 in MCA livery. Not delivered.
	PI-C910					Re-allocated 8/63 for Cruz Airways. Not delivered.
	G-ASKK	Handley Page				Re-registered 17/7/63.
		Autair			8/63	Leased to 12/63.
	PP-ASU	Sadia			6/12/63	Leased.
	G-ASKK	Handley Page			19/10/64	
		BMA			1/2/65	
		BU(CI) Airways			15/2/67	
		BUIA				Re-registered 1/11/68
		BIA				Re-registered 20/7/70.
		Air UK				1/80
162	CF-MCM		210	8/8/62		Converted from series 211. Built for MCA. Not delivered.
	HB-AAG	Globe Air			4/5/63	*Herald of Bern*.
	G-ATHB	Handley Page			22/7/65	
	B-2001	FAT			16/2/66	WFS. Engineless Taipei, Taiwan.
163	G-ASBF	BUA	204	24/9/62	26/11/62	VIP fit.
	G-ASBP					Re-registered for call-sign reasons 27/6/62.
	PI-C869	Air Manila			25/3/66	On two-month lease.
	G-ASBP	Handley Page				Re-registered 16/5/66. Shown at Farnborough 9/66 in Air Manila colours.
	PI-C869	Air Manila			21/10/66	Hangar collapsed at Manila in typhoon 11/70. WFS /72.
164	G-ASBG	Handley Page	203	13/11/62		

	I-TIVA	Itavia			12/4/63	
	G-ASBG	BIA			11/7/73	
		Air UK			1/80	
165	CF-EPA		207	12/12/62		For EPA but not delivered.
	109	RJAF			22/1/63	
	JY-ACR	Alia			12/63	
	G-ATHE	Handley Page			26/7/65	
		BMA			17/8/65	Leased to 15/9/65.
		BU(CI) Airways			/65	Leased. Returned 1966.
	D-BOBO	Bavaria			4/4/66	*Herald of the Alps*.
	G-ATHE	Handley Page			14/10/68	
	B-2011	FAT			19/2/69	WFS. Derelict, Taipei.
166	CF-EPI	EPA	206	27/1/63	13/2/63	
	G-BCWE	BAF			28/1/75	*Jeremy Keegan*.
		Air Anglia			1/4/76	Leased.
		BAF			5/76	
		BIA			1/1/79	L. *Caroline Frost*.
167	CF-EPC	EPA	206	8/3/63	29/3/63	
	VP-BCG	Bahamas Airways			1/2/64	Leased to 5/64.
	CF-EPC	EPA			5/64	
	G-BDFE	BAF			9/75	*Rory Keegan*, VIP fit.
168	I-TIVE	Itavia	203	4/4/63	4/5/63	WO Rome Ciampino 4/71. Parts to BIA.
169	HB-AAH	Globe Air	210	25/7/63	7/8/63	*Herald of Zurich*.
	G-AVEZ	BU(CI) Airways			12/12/66	D still as HB-AAH. Re-registered 17/3/67.
	PP-ASW	Sadia			13/1/68	Leased.
	G-AVEZ	BU(CI) Airways			9/4/68	
		BUIA			1/11/68	
		BIA			20/7/70	
170	110	RJAF	207	26/6/63	12/7/63	
	JY-ACQ	Alia			12/63	WO near Damascus 10/4/65.
171	FM1020	RMAF	401	28/9/63	1/11/63	
	G-BEYD	BAF			18/10/77	*Amy Johnson*.
		Nile Valley Aviation			24/6/78	L. Returned 28/10/78.
		BIA			1/4/79	L.
172	FM1021	RMAF	401	8/11/63	20/12/63	
	G-BEYE	BAF			14/11/77	*Rupert Keegan*.

		Nile Valley Aviation			24/10/78	Leased.
173	HB-AAI		210	18/2/64		Built for Globe Air. Not delivered.
	G-ASPJ	Handley Page			26/2/64	
		Alia			2/64	Leased to 10/3/64.
	HB-AAK	Globe Air			13/3/64	*Herald of Basle*.
	F-OCLY	EAS			18/7/68	
	F-BLOY					Re-registered 5/69.
		Air Inter			8/78	Leased.
174	G-8-2		209	18/4/64		
	4X-AHS	Arkia			18/5/64	
	G-BEZB	Field Aviation			28/7/77	
		Intra Airways				Sold to Intra 1/8/77. Operated in Express Air Freight livery.
		Express Air Services				Now Jersey European Airways.
175	FM1022	RMAF	401	3/1/64	17/1/64	
	G-BEYF	BAF			15/8/77	*Wendela Keegan*.
		Gulf Air				Leased from mid 10/77.
		BIA			1/5/78	Leased.
		BAF				
176	D-BIBI	Bavaria	213	2/4/64	1/5/64	
	G-AVPN	Handley Page			22/6/67	On charter until 30/4/69.
	I-TIVB	Itavia			21/7/67	Sold to Itavia 2/7/70 (previously leased).
	G-AVPN	BIA			13/7/73	
		Air UK			1/80	
177	G-ATIG	Handley Page	214	9/9/65		
	PP-SDI	Sadia			18/9/65	
	G-ATIG	BMA			28/4/73	
		BIA			1/4/75	Leased to 31/10/75.
		Brymon Airways			1/1/77	
178	FM1023	RMAF	401	30/1/64	8/2/64	
	G-BEYG	BAF			12/9/77	All Freight. *Jeremy Keegan*.
179	D-BEBE	Bavaria	213	19/3/65	29/3/65	*Herald of Bavaria*.
		Arkia			24/11/67	Partial livery. L.
	G-AYMG	BIA			13/11/70	
		Air UK			1/80	
180	FM1024	RMAF	401	30/7/64	28/9/64	
	G-BEYH	BAF			18/1/78	

181	FM1025	RMAF	401	22/9/64	3/11/64	WO 17/1/76. Beyond economical repair. Broken up for spares. in Malaysia /78.
	G-BEYI	BAF				NTU.
182	FM1026	RMAF	401	18/11/64	8/12/64	
	G-BEYJ	RAF			22/12/77	
183	G-8-1		209	26/3/64		
	4X-AHR	Arkia			17/4/64	
	G-BAZJ	BIA			6/73	
		Air UK			1/80	
184	I-TIVU	Itavia	203	14/5/64	29/5/64	
	G-BBXI	BIA			20/12/73	
		Air UK			1/80	
185	G-8-3		214	2/7/64		
	G-ASVO	Handley Page			13/8/64	Shown at Farnborough 9/64 in Sadia colours.
	PP-SDG	Sadia			23/10/64	
	G-ASVO	BMA			23/3/73	
		Air Anglia			31/10/75	Leased to 31/3/76.
		BMA			4/76	
		BAF			7/1/77	*Kirsty Keegan*.
		Gulf Air			1/5/77	Leased.
		BAF				Returned.
		BIA			1/1/79	L. Now Air UK.
186	PP-SDH	Sadia	214	5/1/65	26/1/65	
		TransBrasil			/72	*Manana*.
		Transportes Aereos Da Bacia Amazonica (TABA)			/76	Leased.
	G-BEBB	BAF			15/7/76	*Wendela Keegan*, now *Sheila Scott*.
		BIA			1/1/79	L. Now Air UK.
187	FM1027	RMAF	401	18/12/64	11/1/65	
	G-BEYK	BAF			5/3/78	
		BIA			23/3/78	S.
188	HB-AAL	Globe Air	210	11/5/65	18/5/65	*Herald of Inter-Laken*.
	F-OCLZ	EAS			16/7/68	
	F-BOIZ					Re-registered 5/69.
189	G-ATDS	Handley Page	209	12/5/65		For operation by BUA in Sadia livery.
	4X-AHT	Arkia			28/7/65	

	G-ATDS	Field Aviation			28/7/77	
		Intra Airways				Sold to Intra 1/8/77. Operated in Express Air Freight livery.
		Express Air Services				Now Jersey European Airways.
190	PP-SDJ	Sadia	214	2/11/65	7/12/65	WO Marumbi Peak 3/11/67.
191	PP-SDL	Sadia	214	3/1/66	1/2/66	
		TransBrasil			/72	
		TABA			/76	Leased.
	G-BDZV	BAF			30/6/76	*Kevin Keegan*,
					22/8/77	L Dan-Air, returned.
		BIA			1/1/79	L. Now Air UK.
192	PI-C866	Air Manila	215	5/3/66	18/3/66	
	RP-C866				/74	WFS.

193 – Airframe used for water tank pressure testing. Sc /70.

194	PP-SDN	Sadia	214	28/12/67	10/1/68	
	G-BAVX	BMA			28/4/73	
		BAF			13/1/77	*Timothy Keegan*.
		Nile Valley Aviation			17/8/77	
		BAF			27/6/78	
195	4X-AHO	Arkia	209	5/4/68	10/4/68	
	G-BFRJ	Field Aircraft			30/3/74	
		Express Air Freight				
		Express Air Services				
		Air Ecosse			11/6/78	Leased.
		Express Air Services			8/9/78	Now Jersey European Airways.
196	I-TIVI	Itavia	203	25/6/68	4/7/68	
	G-BBXJ	BIA			18/12/73	WO Jersey 24/12/74. Wings in BIA hangar Southampton. Fuselage still at Jersey (in fire service training yard). Brown c/s.
197	4X-AHN	Arkia	209	13/8/68	16/8/68	
	G-BFRK	Field Aircraft			6/4/78	
		Express Air Freight				
		Express Air Services				Now Jersey European Airways.

252 - Components only - airframes not completed.
257 - Laid down 1964 as series 700 for VASP. Cancelled 1966.

HERALD FLYING HOURS AND LANDINGS DECEMBER 7, 1978

Const. No.	Reg'n.	Operator	Hours	Landgs.	Date Recorded	First Flight	Delivery Date
149	G-APWA	BAF	22,316	24,145	Oct 31 78	Oct 30 59	Nov 19 66
153	G-APWE	BIA	27,325	34,459	Oct 31 78	Dec 13 61	Jan 4 62
151	HK-715	Urraca	18,845	18,409	May 24 75	Nov 2 61	Jan 5 62
159	G-BCZG	BAF	22,480	36,972	Oct 31 78	Jan 15 62	Feb 13 62
154	G-APWF	BIA	26,667	33,375	Oct 31 78	Mar 29 62	Apr 9 62
155	G-APWG	BIA	26,864	34,047	Oct 31 78	Apr 27 62	May 22 62
156	G-APWH	BIA	26,682	33,127	Oct 31 78	May 23 62	Jun 6 62
165	B-2011	FAT	10,550	8,884	July 27 76	Dec 21 62	Jan 22 63
166	G-BCWE	BAF	24,233	29,417	Oct 31 78	Jan 27 63	Feb 13 63
167	G-BDFE	BAF	22,774	28,504	Oct 31 78	Mar 8 63	Mar 29 63
164	G-ASBG	BIA	25,516	29,261	Oct 31 78	Nov 13 62	Apr 12 63
162	B-2001	FAT	12,264	10,868	July 27 76	Aug 8 62	Feb 16 66
158	G-APWJ	BIA	25,305	31,629	Oct 31 78	May 29 63	Jun 13 63
169	G-AVEZ	BIA	26,671	30,175	Oct 31 78	Jul 25 63	Aug 6 63
171	G-BEYD	BAF	9,781	6,625	Oct 31 78	Sep 28 63	Nov 1 63
172	G-BEYE	BAF	10,637	7,162	Oct 31 78	Nov 8 63	Dec 20 63
175	G-BEYF	BAF	10,175	7,830	Oct 31 78	Jan 3 64	Jan 17 64
178	G-BEYG	BAF	8,162	5,283	Oct 31 78	Jan 30 64	Feb 8 64
173	F-BLOY	EAS	15,903	9,664	Sept 30 78	Feb 18 64	Mar 13 64
183	G-BAZJ	BIA	24,279	30,967	Oct 31 78	Mar 26 64	Apr 17 64
176	G-AVPN	BIA	23,198	25,084	Oct 31 78	Apr 2 64	May 1 64
174	G-BEZB	Field A/C	20,946	26,218	Nov 29 78	Apr 18 64	May 18 64
184	G-BBXI	BIA	24,384	28,034	Oct 31 78	May 14 64	May 29 64
180	G-BEYH	BAF	9,000	5,858	Oct 31 78	Jul 30 64	Sep 28 64
185	G-ASVO	BAF	22,667	25,660	Oct 31 78	Jul 2 64	Oct 6 64
182	G-BEYJ	BAF	9,947	6,628	Oct 31 78	Nov 18 64	Dec 8 64
187	G-BEYK	BIA	7,808	5,254	Oct 31 78	Dec 18 64	Jan 11 65
186	G-BEBB	BAF	26,306	27,868	Oct 31 78	Jan 5 65	Jan 26 65
161	G-ASKK	BIA	25,465	31,250	Oct 31 78	Jul 5 62	Feb 1 65
179	G-AYMG	BIA	22,711	24,325	Oct 31 78	Mar 19 65	Mar 29 65

Const. No.	Reg'n.	Operator	Hours	Landgs.	Date Recorded	First Flight	Delivery Date
188	F-BOIZ	EAS	14,334	9,007	Nov 8 78	May 11 65	May 18 65
189	G-ATDS	Field A/C	18,118	22,794	Nov 29 78	Jun 30 65	Jul 28 65
177	G-ATIG	Brymon Airways	22,107	23,787	Oct 31 78	Sep 9 65	Sep 18 65
191	G-BDZV	BAF	21,707	22,789	Oct 31 78	Jan 3 66	Feb 1 66
192	RP-C866	Air Manila	12,388	10,213	May 10 78	Mar 5 66	Mar 19 66
194	G-BAVX	BAF	16,794	18,059	Oct 31 78	Dec 28 67	Jan 11 68
195	G-BFRJ	Field A/C	16,207	20,278	Nov 23 78	Apr 5 68	Apr 10 68
197	G-BFRK	Field A/C	15,342	19,462	Nov 29 78	Aug 13 68	Aug 16 68

Total: Flying Hours: 806,114 Landings: 894,411